The Independent Pensioner

Financial Strategies for an Affluent Retirement

The Independent Pensioner

Financial Strategies for an Affluent Retirement

by

Anthony Vice

RIGHT WAY
plus

Typeset in 10½/11½ pt Legacy by Letterpart Ltd., Reigate, Surrey.

Printed and bound in Great Britain by Mackays of Chatham.

The *Right Way Plus* series is published by Elliot Right Way Books, Brighton Road, Lower Kingswood, Tadworth, Surrey, KT20 6TD, U.K. For information about our company and the other books we publish, visit our website at www.right-way.co.uk

Dedication

For Elizabeth and Susan, John, Philippa

Contents

Preface

The parties are over. You have been given, accompanied by some well-chosen words, the gold watch – or nowadays the personal organiser. You have handed over your files, cleared your desk and reviewed all your outstanding jobs with your successor and your other colleagues. The following Monday, you do not go to the office. You have retired.

The financial characteristics of being retired are essentially very simple. Your income, your standard of living and by implication your assets, are largely fixed. You have virtually no control over your pension, which will be determined by trustees, an insurance company or the State. You can no longer go to your employer and negotiate an increase in income. You have left the employment market. It is possible to go back, but it may not be easy to find another job to improve your living standards.

Assuming that you enjoy average health, retirement at age 60 will leave you a further 19 years by the actuarial averages for men. Women can expect to live 5 years longer. You will have to deal with general inflation; even at 2.5% a year – the target which has been given to the Bank of England – a £100 bill will have risen to £160 by the end of 19 years. And you should prudently assume that the costs of healthcare, domestic help and accommodation will rise faster than the average.

If you have worked for central or local government, you may have a fully-indexed pension, where the payments increase in line with retail prices. If you have worked in the private sector as an employee, or self-employed, you may perhaps have arranged a fully-indexed pension with an insurance company. The money you receive from this will keep up with prices – though with a time-lag.

If you have worked in the private sector, you are most unlikely to receive a fully-indexed pension. Assuming you receive a company pension, like so many people, you will find that the trustees meet once a year and determine an increase in your pension. The trustees have a legal obligation to raise your pension (at least for recent years) in line with inflation – so again there is a time-lag – but only up to 5% a year. If inflation rises above that level, as it did in the late 1970s and early 1980s, you cannot rely on any further protection for your income.

This book is intended to help pensioners who have some degree of flexibility in their financial affairs to manage their income and capital, so that over the years they can gain the maximum possible benefit.

Anthony Vice

Chapter 1:

Introduction

Starting Your Pension

You will have started thinking about your pension, and discussing it, some time before your retirement date. The principal differences in approach lie between employees in a company scheme and the self-employed (which may include people who are employed, but have no company scheme and have made independent arrangements); you also need to take into account your State pension.

For Employees

Some months before you retire, you will have agreed the date and amount of your pension, probably in face to face meetings or by inter-office memos with your personnel manager or a pension fund representative. Shortly before your retirement date you will get a letter from your employer setting out your pension situation in the light of the decisions which you have taken and been agreed. The letter will show:

❖ The amount of your pension and the date from which it is to be paid. If you have been making AVC payments (Additional Voluntary Contributions) these will also be included.

❖ The timing of your pension payments (typically the 15th of the month) and when the pension trustees will meet each year to consider possible pension increases.

❖ Details of the widow's/widower's pension if you die first and a statement of the payments which will be made should you die early after your retirement.

❖ A statement regarding cash commutation – whether, as is to be hoped, you are taking in cash the maximum 25% of

11

the total fund which the Inland Revenue allows you, or whether you have opted to take the annual pension at its full value.

Look at each of these points in turn. The amount of your pension will already have been discussed and agreed. If you are in a final salary scheme, it will represent up to two-thirds of your final salary (carefully defined by the Inland Revenue rules to allow for benefits in kind, such as a company car) for the time you have worked spread over the 20, 30 or maybe even 40 years as laid down in the pension scheme rules.

If you are in a money-purchase or defined contribution scheme, then the amount of your pension will represent an actuarial value of the total worth of your pension assets assessed against the prevailing annuity rates. If the pension figure is different from what you had expected, ask at once and in writing. You should react in the same way if the AVC total differs from what you had expected.

This book is not aimed at pre-retirement, but it is to be hoped that you did make some AVC payments, particularly in the years leading up to retirement. The Inland Revenue allows you to set aside 15% of your income in AVC and pension payments. If you are a member of a non-contributory scheme, you can therefore commit 15% of your income and this payment is tax-deductible. You can invest the AVC in your employer's pension fund or set up a Free Standing AVC with a bank or insurance company. The advantage is evident from this example: suppose you put £1,000 into an AVC the year before your retirement; if you pay higher rate tax the cost to you would be £600. On retirement, you can take 25% or £250 in cash so that the net cost to you then stands at £350. And for that £350 you have a pension fund worth £750 (the original £1,000 less the cash taken) so that even if annuity rates are low, as they have been over recent years, you are more than doubling your return over a short period of time.

The timing of pension payments should not be a major issue. Payments should be made to you monthly, as your salary was paid – and a pension is deferred salary. Most pensions are paid in the middle of the month – a compromise because to pay at the end of the month would give the pension provider a cash flow advantage, while to pay at the beginning of the month would give you an advantage. Payment will be made into your nominated bank account and you may receive each month a statement showing the gross pension, the amount of tax deducted and the net sum paid into your bank account. Keep these monthly statements to compare them with the P60 form which you will receive after the end of the financial year. Also check with your bank statement to make sure there is no time-lag in the net pension getting into your account. If there is a delay, contact the pension provider: cash flow is important!

Terms of the widow's/widower's pension are self-evidently important. If you are a married man, you are actuarially expected to pre-decease your spouse (assuming you are older or both of similar age), when a modified pension will be paid to her. The same arrangement should work for two unmarried partners (if the pension fund has rules which pose a problem, you may need legal advice). Is this what you want? For most people it will be, but if you want to modify the arrangements – say to provide for a disabled child – then you need to sit down with the pension provider and have the modified arrangements set out in writing. Your first consideration should be whether the pension for widow/widower is adequate. Pension schemes typically provide a half or two-thirds (the permitted maximum) for the survivor. You must consider whether this will be sufficient; if you feel it may not be enough, one option is to talk to your pension fund about a reduction in your own pension in return for a higher payment to the survivor. If the amount involved is significant, then you should go to a pension adviser. You also need to think about other dependants, say your children. In a typical occupational final salary scheme, the half to two-thirds pension will stop on the second death, i.e. that of the survivor. The self-employed, who have to make their own arrangements with an insurance company, can obtain greater flexibility. Former employees need to reflect on dependants' needs, and this may affect their will and lifetime gifts.

One final point in your letter is what will happen if you die within a short time of retiring. Generally, the letter will say that if you die within five years of your retirement date then your pension will be paid in full for that period. In the jargon, your pension is being paid "five years certain". Self-employed have to decide for themselves how long this period should be, and the number of years is reflected in the terms. For former employees, this should form part of your letter. If for some reason this certain period is not offered, then you should consider whether to make your own arrangements – a good deal will depend on the payments position for widows/widowers.

WHAT YOU ARE NOT TOLD

That covers your typical pension letter for ex-employees. But what is left out is at least as important, perhaps even more, than what is included. The first omission is tax. The letter will simply state that your pension of £x000 a year will be paid for life "subject to income tax". This begs the question: will it be the right amount of tax? You should talk to your accounts department and, if there are complexities, it may be worth going to an accountant for an expert view. One reason for concern is the evidence that the Inland Revenue has become slower and less accurate since the introduction of self-assessment, featuring in headline-grabbing stories of computer glitches in tax offices. The second, and related, reason is that there may be tax changes which arise when you cease to be an employee. You may have been provided with a 'perk' such as a car together with fuel for private use. Those benefits will have been added to your taxable income for the coding which the Inland Revenue supplies and which the pension fund will use when it deducts tax from your monthly pension. These benefits will stop when you retire, so that your coding should change. In time, the Revenue will catch up with all this, but for the sake of your cash flow it is sensible to ensure that your tax coding is altered in your favour as soon as possible.

Even more important for most pensioners is how their income will be protected against rising prices. Your letter may simply state that the trustees will meet annually to review or consider pensions. In fact, your position is somewhat better than that, though some pension providers may not feel the need to spell out the trustees' legal obligations. In short, these are to provide limited price indexation (LPI) for pensions built up from April 1997 onwards; this means that each year pensions must be increased in line with inflation up to a maximum of 5%. Later in this book the question will be addressed as to what pensioners can do if inflation rises above 5%.

The good side of LPI, as it is known, is that employers may apply the mandatory increase to all pensioners which will give indexation in times of low inflation. The less good side is that the increases come in arrears, so that a pensioner could, for example, have endured inflation for a year before his pension is corrected.

The other less good side is that inflation is defined as price inflation – changes in the level of retail prices – as opposed to earnings inflation which has been consistently higher for many years past (which explains, for example, why State pensioners do so badly compared with average earnings and why a growing proportion of people are paying higher rate tax – the tax allowances are lagging behind incomes).

For the Self-Employed

The self-employed's pension rights will be a lump sum, accumulated with an insurance company or unitised funds. The first question is whether to take cash, which can represent up to 25% of the total fund. In the great majority of cases, the answer must be YES! Most people can find a use for a cash lump sum, which is tax-free and can be used in any way the pensioner wishes; it is even possible to buy an annuity which comes on more favourable tax terms than the sort you have to buy at age 75 (the compulsory purchase annuity).

The second important question for the self-employed man or woman is what sort of annuity to choose. This decision has to reflect a number of factors – age, health and dependants. The highest annual income will come from a 'level' annuity, where the amount of money paid is fixed for your life.

A period of certain payments will reduce the annual annuity payment, but the big difference comes if you want to base the annuity on joint lives, i.e. make sure that some or even the same annuity is paid to your spouse after your death. The other major difference arises if, instead of a level annuity, you opt for annual increases of 3%, 5%, or even in line with (price) inflation. Inflation-linking has only become an effective option in recent years, with the fall in the headline rate. A whole range opens up: at one extreme, a level annuity on one life payable for three years certain; at the other extreme, an annuity on joint lives (ten years certain) linked to inflation. The choice has to depend on the individual's aims and circumstances; but do discuss your decision, especially within the family, before you commit. See Chapter 3.

Buying an annuity has become much simpler nowadays. Brief

tables of rates offered by different insurance companies are now published in the weekend newspapers. If you have access to the internet, a decision can sensibly be made unless your affairs are complex or unless you have a specific requirement. Should you feel that you do need expert advice, a number of financial advisers can help at a reduced rate of commission. If you need to go to a specialist and put questions to actuaries, you could expect to pay commission.

Some of these choices involve investment decisions which will be dealt with later in this book. If a self-employed man takes 25% cash from his pension fund, we have seen that he can use that to buy an annuity on better terms than on the mandatory part. Or he could invest the 25% in bonds or shares. The annuity will die with him (subject to years certain), but that may matter little if he does not have dependants. But neither can he change his mind, once he is committed to a specific annuity plan.

It has been assumed in this book that the self-employed, or the holder of a money purchase scheme, will decide to retire at 60. Under present legislation, he has until 75 before he has to take a final financial decision. Being compelled to take an annuity by this specific time, especially if annuity rates are then looking unfavourable, has seemed unreasonable to many commentators. As a result, income drawdown has emerged (discussed in more detail in Chapter 3): this is an alternative to buying an annuity, under which income is drawn directly from the pool of funds, under official guidelines: income must be no more than an annuity for a single person and must not be less than 35% of that maximum figure. The attraction of income drawdown is that it gives flexibility on timing, so that one does not have to buy an annuity when one's assets are temporarily depressed in value and/or annuity rates are unfavourable. The drawback is that income drawdown is rather cumbersome, therefore costly, and so far has been confined to relatively large amounts of pension assets. And the government threatens to change the rules on drawdown, adversely affecting pensioners from 2004.

State Pension

For men retiring at 60, the State retirement pension is not a current issue: the pension is paid at retirement age, at present 65 for men and 60 for women, though women's pension age is in the process of being increased to 65: women born after March 1955 will not receive a State pension until the age of 65. A married couple can qualify for a higher pension based on the husband's national insurance record. The State pension needs to be considered, if only for cash flow assessment. It can be paid into a bank account, weekly in advance, and is taxable. The State does not deduct tax nor does it issue P60s at the end of the financial year. The Inland Revenue gets its tax by deduction through the coding system, where the code reflects the State pension and is attached to the principal source of your income.

Your Entitlement to Information

In terms of information, the only entitlement of the self-employed is that the insurance company provide a P60 at the end of the financial year. He needs to check that the monthly or quarterly transfer is reaching his bank account; he may well not receive a separate notification. The ex-employee is rather better placed, and should see his pension fund's annual report or statement of affairs. That report should include the names of the trustees, the actuary, investment adviser and details of the fund's assets; it will also contain a record of recent years' pension increases. It is a good idea to keep the latest report, so that names are available to whom a query can be addressed. If you have a specialist query, you may find the fund's actuary is prepared to assist on an informal basis. Ex-employees may also have a slight edge over the self-employed as they are often entitled to concessions related to their former employer's business – concessions on motor or house insurance, travel concessions and so on. In a perfect world, the personnel department would make these known, but people are busy; so ask.

Income Tax

The UK tax system consists, essentially, of indirect taxes on goods and services (such as VAT, Excise Duty) and three direct taxes – income tax, capital gains tax and inheritance tax. Everyone who has retired will have paid income tax – a great deal during his working life – and knows how it operates.

The biggest change on retirement is that your income is lower – which is considered in the section on investment. But there are two other changes to the tax system: if you were employed, or working under contract, you no longer have help from the accounts department which stood between you and the Inland Revenue. Secondly, the tax system offers some benefits for older people – but also some traps for the unwary.

Taxable v Tax-free

For many retired people, a typical situation is that the husband receives an employer's pension, or frequently more than one, plus the State pension (if he is over 65) and some income from investments; his wife will probably receive a smaller State pension plus some investment income.

The first steps are to identify income which is not taxable, to make sure that the Inland Revenue gets its figures right, and to deal with situations which would push up your tax bill. Tax-free income covers a range of benefits, such as attendance allowance and the winter fuel payment which is made to pensioners. Much of National Savings are tax-free, such as certificates and premium bonds, as are the gains and income from ISAs and PEPs. Also free of current tax at present is the 5% a year which you can withdraw from an insurance bond – but this may change following the Sandler report of mid-2002, which recommended the ending of this 5% a year concession along with the creation of low-cost, simplified investment products.

Net v Gross

Most of the income you receive will arrive net of tax, though there will be more tax to pay if you are a higher-rate payer. Your pension from your former employer will reach you net under coding (discussed later); bank interest will come after tax at 20% while share dividends will be paid net of a 10% tax credit. Now you have retired, it could be important to establish where non-taxpayers can reclaim tax and where they cannot. Tax on bank interest can be reclaimed or you can arrange to have it paid gross. But the tax credit on share dividends cannot be reclaimed (except for the present in an ISA): that was the important change made by Gordon Brown which meant that pension funds could no longer reclaim tax – so reducing the value of everyone's pension fund.

Gross income (where no tax has been deducted) is less usual. If you have income from property or are self-employed, your income will come to you gross but you will have to pay tax later. Your State pension is paid gross but is subject to tax. Maintenance income, if you are divorced or separated, will be paid without any deduction for tax and normally will not count as part of your taxable income.

Tax Reliefs

You have now established your total income, from April 6 to April 5 in the next calendar year. As a first step to establish your tax bill, you deduct the reliefs. (Note: the term 'total income' has a specific meaning, namely your income after reliefs; this is an important term we come across later.)

When you were employed, and contributed to your employer's pension scheme, you were given relief on these payments. Now you are retired, the most significant relief will probably be your gifts to charity, which you make net of basic rate tax and will reduce your tax bill if you are a higher-rate payer. There is limited relief if you were 65 in April 2000 and are making maintenance payments to a former spouse. You also get relief on 20% of the investment you make in an Enterprise Investment Scheme or a Venture Capital Trust.

Allowances

You have now established your total income. In order to reach your taxable income, you have to deduct your allowances. These are mainly age-related, and this is an important area for pensioners; there are benefits but some traps. The two principal allowances are your personal allowance and the married couple's allowance; for 2003-4 these have been set as follows:

Personal:	Under 65	£4,615
	65–74	£6,610
	75 plus	£6,720
Married Couple:	68–74 – 10% of	£5,565
	75 plus – 10% of	£5,635

(Married couple's allowance is available only where one spouse was aged 65 or more in April 2000. Tax relief in this case represents 10% of the allowance.) All the allowances for pensioners mentioned in this chapter are likely to be uprated annually.

There are also allowances for people who are registered as blind and there are children's tax credits.

IMPROVED BY AGE – BUT RESTRICTED BY INCOME

These improvements for older taxpayers are reduced if your income rises above a certain level: if the husband's total income (income after reliefs) is £18,300 or more, his personal allowance is reduced by £1 for each extra £2 of income which is over the limit until he receives the same allowance as the under-65s – that is the minimum. So if he is in the 65-74 age bracket, his allowance will be reduced to the minimum once it has risen to £22,290.

Look closely at this trap: as your income rises, and you lose your allowance, you are paying a high marginal tax rate – around 30%. Once your income has passed this point, your marginal tax rate goes back to the normal rate of 22%. There are two ways to avoid this period of high tax: if your rising income is coming from investments, then look at moving some to your spouse or holding them in joint names. (This also has benefits for capital gains tax and inheritance tax.) If you have some flexibility in arranging how your income rises, then consider National Savings certificates or ISAs.

USING ALLOWANCES

Children's tax credits – available if you have a child or children under 16 living with you – have recently been changed. The new Child Tax Credit, which must be claimed, is paid direct to the wife or partner as the responsible carer, not as before to the father. Most families with children are eligible: for families with two children the credit is worth £3,405 at an annual income of £15,000, dropping sharply to £545 when your income improves to £25,000 – and falling further to £210 when your income reaches £55,000. (The credit is available to all families having an income of less than £58,000.) Remember: you have to ask.

Your Tax Bill

You have established your income, you have deducted your reliefs and from that you have deducted your allowances. The balance is your taxable income, and this is taxed at the following rates:

Up to £1,960   10% (starting rate)
£1,961 to £30,500   22% (basic rate)
Over £30,500   40% (higher rate)

There are a number of consequent tax rates, such as 10% deducted from dividends and 32.5% higher rate on dividends. For perhaps half of all retired people, the amount of tax you have to pay is organised through your annual return. Some points on filling in your return are set out on pages 24–27.

Tax Coding

If you receive an employer's pension, you will normally receive your income after tax has been deducted. The way this works is that the Inland Revenue gives your pension provider a tax code, aiming to deduct the right amount of tax from your pension – if you receive more than one pension, the coding will go to the principal supplier, then to the others.

You will get a coding notice soon after the start of the new tax year on April 6, and you should look at this carefully. (If you don't receive a notice, you should assume that the Inland Revenue is using the same code as the previous year.) Your code will consist of a letter and a number: the letters should be explained in the accompanying notice, so that for example BR means that tax is collected at the basic rate, and K means that you have negative allowances, because your untaxed income exceeds your personal allowances.

WHAT TO CHECK – AND WHAT TO NOTIFY

You should look at the arithmetic in the coding notice; you need to be sure that you have been given the correct allowances and that the offsets against your allowances – your State pension and other income – are right. Check that you have the right code letter. On your side, you need to notify the Inland Revenue when your tax situation changes. They should have your date of birth, to give you higher allowances when you reach 65 and 75 – but, as always, check. You need to tell them if your spouse dies or if you become divorced or separated.

Increasing Your Income

Probably the biggest single change for most people on retirement is their fall in income – even if you receive the maximum permitted of your final salary. People therefore look for ways to increase their cash inflow, and one of the most popular is through letting. Buy-to-let is discussed in a later chapter, but you can simply let out a furnished room in your home. Under the rent a room scheme, you can receive £4,250 of rent a year free of tax, though if this is new to you, you may need advice. You have to live in the property, which must be your main home and you cannot offset expenses: you have the usual option of offsetting expenses against the rent you receive as an alternative.

If you own a second home, there is the alternative of a furnished holiday letting (described more fully in the section on buy-to-let). If you can satisfy the conditions, this offers a number of advantages as the Inland Revenue treat it as a business. That means you get more favourable capital gains treatment when you sell and you can claim pension payments and capital allowances against the income. Business assets also receive more favourable treatment under inheritance tax.

National Insurance and Council Tax

National Insurance, whatever politicians may say, is a tax: Class 4 contributions do not entitle you to any State benefits. Happily for the great majority of pensioners, people over the State pension age are excluded – 60 for women (at present) and 65 for men. National Insurance remains an important issue if you employ people or if you are self-employed, and pre-retirement people will need specialist advice.

Council tax, which represents an important outgoing for many retired people, concerns local authorities rather than the Inland Revenue. This tax is based on the value of a property and partly on the people who live there: all domestic properties are currently allocated to one of eight bands, depending on their value, and taxed accordingly. There are benefits to reduce council tax, but not if you have savings above a modest level. Probably the most relevant discount, of 25% for living alone, does not depend on savings or income.

Keeping Income Tax Down

Different ways to reduce, or even escape, tax are reviewed throughout this book, but there are some basic suggestions regarding income tax:

❖ Use your allowances; they cannot be claimed back. Consider transferring assets, especially shares and others which produce income.

❖ Organise your giving to charity. Make sure that all donations are made by way of Gift Aid and remember that you can give shares free of capital gains tax.

❖ Think about a stakeholder pension as a way of saving, even after you have retired, so long as you are not yet 75; it will not reduce your income tax bill but it will give you a significant tax benefit.

❖ If you put money on deposit, think about going offshore, e.g. to Eire. You will be paid gross and you can arrange over a year's delay before you pay the tax. This is good for your cash flow, but remember that UK compensation schemes do not apply.

❖ If you worked for a company which provided shares under profit-sharing, make use of the concessions to put them into an ISA or a stakeholder pension: talk to the company secretary or accounts.

❖ Keep records – if possible for up to six years. You have an obligation to keep records, but this is for your own benefit if you are challenged by the Inland Revenue or if they carry out an enquiry, which they can do on a random basis.

❖ Appeal. You have rights against the Inland Revenue, if you think that you are being treated wrongly or unusually slowly or even without proper courtesy. And in the last analysis you can go for help to your MP.

Your Tax Return

Filling in your tax return is the crux of the financial year. This intimidating document, or series of documents, will reflect all of your tax reduction schemes; above all, it will show how much tax you will have to pay.

To guide you in detail through completing your tax return would take a book in itself – and there are several which do the job. Here are ten points which you need to consider when completing your return, or when your adviser or accountant does the work for you.

I.   Who gets a return?

When you fill in your return, you are being assessed under the tax system of self-assessment. Perhaps half of all retired people will be sent a return: if you pay tax at higher rate, if you are self-employed, if you receive untaxed income or if your tax affairs are at all complicated. If you are not sent a return, but make a capital gain or have a new source of income, you have six months after the end of the financial year to tell the Inspector; he will then send you a return to complete.

II.   Is your return complete?

You should receive the return itself, plus supplementary pages which relate to your own circumstances, plus a guide to completing your return plus a tax calculation guide – there is also a longer comprehensive tax calculation guide. If any of these documents are missing, above all the supplementary pages, then you need to contact the Inland Revenue.

III.   Rounding

Some people make it a point of principle to round down their income to the nearest pound and to round up their expenses to the nearest pound (they probably pay their bills by second-class post and send credits to their bank by first-class post). There is nothing wrong with this procedure, which can save useful amounts over time. The Inspector has the option, after all, of re-working your figures or using pounds and pence together.

IV.   PAYE payment

If you are under PAYE and owe tax of less than £2,000, you will be given a choice. The tax will normally be collected through the PAYE system, but you can opt to pay it as a lump sum. Unless you have some particular reason, it makes sense for your tax to be collected through PAYE: this is spread throughout the year, so that in effect you are being offered a 12-month interest-free reducing loan of the amount of the tax. It will almost always make sense to take the loan.

V.   State pension

You will discover, if you were not already aware, that the State does not issue P60 forms. You should keep a record of the amount you receive, which is easy if you have your pension paid into the bank. There is a slight anomaly in the tax treatment: the amount on which you are taxed is the amount you would have been paid had you chosen to receive your pension weekly. Now you can arrange to have your pension paid weekly into a bank; you have to ask. You need, as ever, to check what you receive – under-payment happens from time to time. You will then be paid your arrears together with a modest rate of interest; the cheerful side is that, in general, interest from government bodies comes free of tax.

VI.   Cashbacks

This is one of the greyer areas in tax. People who buy ISAs and unit trusts are frequently offered cashbacks by buying through a discount broker. ISAs do not enter into the tax system; for unit trusts the Inland Revenue seems prepared to ignore the income benefit, on the basis that the cashback is used to reduce the cost of your acquisition – and therefore increase the capital gain when you come to sell. For cars and mortgages the amounts are larger. You should ask the company which gives you the incentive and keep their letter or make a note of their telephone reply; if you employ an adviser or an accountant, tell him or her.

VII.   Working out your tax

You have a choice here: you can ask the Inland Revenue to calculate your tax, in which case you need to deliver your return together with the supplementary pages, by 30 September. Alternatively, you can work out your own tax and in that case you need to send your return plus supplementary pages and your tax calculation by 31 January of the following year. There is a view that you should not try to work out your own tax but leave the Inland Revenue to do the work and carry the responsibility for any errors and omissions. You should certainly form a rough estimate of your tax liability and be prepared to take action if the Inland Revenue figure comes in much larger.

VIII. *Widowers*

Widows' bereavement allowance was ended for death of husbands after April 2000; there has never until recently been a widower's allowance in the UK tax system. But if you are a widower whose wife died during the six years up to April 2000, it may be worthwhile putting a claim to the Inland Revenue for an amount equal to the widows' bereavement allowance (using the Human Rights Act).

IX.   *Accumulation unit trusts*

Many people, especially when seeking to build up capital, buy accumulation units in unit trusts; in these units, the dividends are not paid out to you (as they would be for income shares) but re-invested. This re-investment can take place in two ways – either enlarging the value of your units or used to buy further units. There are two traps waiting here for the unwary: the first is that you have to account for the dividend, which counts as your income whether or not it is paid out to you – it is your property. Secondly, you have to note the acquisition costs and dates in order to work out capital gains tax when you sell the units. This results in an unwieldy calculation, but you can always ask the unit trust manager for confirmation of your figures.

X.   *Sign*

Do not forget to sign and date your return; a surprising number of people do forget, possibly because that section is not made very prominent. An unsigned return is not acceptable to the

Inland Revenue, and, if you do forget, it may take an unusually long time for the return to come back to you. You must keep a copy of all your communications with the Inland Revenue and it is a good idea to confirm in a letter the upshot of any telephone conversation. When you write to the Inland Revenue on something of importance, do use recorded delivery. For less than £1 you can send a letter which has to be signed for; no-one can plead 'lost in the post'.

Capital Gains Tax (CGT)

You pay capital gains tax whenever you sell or give away something you own – the main exception being your own home. Transfers between spouses do not rank for capital gains tax and every year every taxpayer has a tax-free allowance for capital gains: any gains which you make up to that amount are free of capital gains tax. For 2003-4 the allowance has been set at £7,900.

For many taxpayers it is possible – as we shall soon see – to avoid paying capital gains tax. But for those who do pay, it is charged at your top rate: higher rate taxpayers pay 40% and a standard rate taxpayer may be pushed into the higher rate band by the size of his capital gain. The other bad news is that CGT is a complicated tax.

When Do You Pay?

Capital gains tax arises on disposal, which is not a precise term but means when you sell or give away something or exchange it for something else. This is the first point at which to pause: if you give shares to your grandson, you are considered to have sold the shares at the prevailing current market price and you have a potential tax liability. There are a few circumstances where capital gains tax does not arise. These exceptions are important – the first, as we have seen, being gifts between husband and wife unless they are separated. Nor does CGT arise on death. (Inheritance tax may apply then if the total estate is above the threshold. When you inherit an asset, you inherit it at the value when your benefactor died.) And gifts to charity are free of gains tax – which can form a useful part of tax planning. Another word of caution: as these transactions are outside CGT, they are free of gains tax – but neither can you claim losses made on such disposals against gains made elsewhere.

Tax-free Gains – and Losses

There are a number of assets which are free of gains (and where, again, you cannot claim losses). Most important is your own home, or principal residence in the jargon: a second or holiday home, however, will be subject to tax. Note that a husband and wife who are together can have only one principal residence; if you buy a second home you can nominate which of the two is principal. In theory, a married couple is worse off in this respect than a couple who co-habit who could each have a principal residence. Private cars are also exempt from CGT as are personal effects ("chattels") which are sold for less than £6,000. ISAs and PEPs are also exempt from CGT, as are gilts and National Savings. Betting and the lottery are outside CGT, along with any gains you make on foreign currency which is for your personal use; also assets gifted to charity; wasting assets which have a useful life of 50 years or less, such as an aeroplane, boat or caravan; gains from the sale of timber and uncut trees, and compensation which you received for an injury or wrong to yourself in a personal capacity, or compensation for bad investment advice which you were given in relation to buying a personal pension in certain specified years.

Joint Holdings for Married Couples

A husband and wife who are together are treated as two separate people, so that each has the year's tax-free allowance. This is an important point for tax planning – for CGT and income tax. If you hold assets, such as shares or valuable belongings such as paintings, which you may want to sell, then there is a clear and powerful case for putting them into joint ownership because you effectively double your tax-free allowance. The Inland Revenue will assume that joint ownership means a 50-50 split, unless you tell them otherwise. In cases where it may be difficult to arrange joint ownership, say with overseas shares, then you can arrange a deed of trust which has the same effect. Remember also a formal point: as husband and wife are separate entities for CGT (as they are for income tax) then each is technically responsible for settling his or her own CGT bill.

Tax on Trusts

Trustees are also liable for CGT if they sell assets in the trust. The rate is set at 34%, i.e. rather below the figure for a higher rate taxpayer, while the tax-free allowance is normally half that applicable to individuals. There are concessions, for example affecting trusts set up for the disabled; this is a specialist area on which you should take advice.

Working Out Your Gain – or Loss

This is where CGT becomes complicated, but you need to make this calculation before you dispose of any substantial asset. You want to avoid paying unnecessary CGT and you also want to make maximum use of the tax-free allowance which is available each year – which is lost if you do not use it.

This forms an important part of CGT strategy: many people have a portfolio of shares acquired some years earlier which they will want to start selling in say five years' time. What they should do in the interim is use the annual allowance (preferably doubled with their spouse) to raise the CGT base as discussed further on pages 34 and 35, so that tax on the eventual disposals is reduced or even made non-existent.

Selling Shares

At this point, you have to go through the calculation process – which is complex, but which may well save you 40% on your gains in a few years' time.

Assume, just to make things simple, that you want to sell a block of shares which you bought a number of years ago – and you are doing this in advance of the actual sale to make sure that you and your spouse stay within the annual tax-free limit. (There are different rules for shares which were bought before 1982 and before 1965.) You need to take a series of steps:

❖ Establish the selling price and deduct the broker's commission (you now have the net proceeds).

❖   Find the cost – you will need the contract note – including brokerage and any other charges.

❖   Offset any expenses you incurred while owning the shares – if you placed them with a bank for safekeeping, for example, you are entitled to offset this charge, thus reducing your gain.

You have now established your net gain – for simplicity's sake, it is being assumed for the moment that this is your only CGT transaction during the financial year. The next step is to deduct the permitted allowances against your net gain. There are two in this case: indexation and taper relief.

Indexing

If you bought an asset before April 1998 then you can deduct the growth of inflation until then (this was on the theory that purely inflationary gains should not be taxed). Suppose that you had bought the shares in December 1996; you can then reduce your gain by the percentage rise in prices from that time until April 1998. The price rise was about 5%, so you increase the cost of your shares by that amount.

You have now established your gain on the shares. If it falls within the annual allowance – single or joint with your spouse – then you know that you have no CGT to pay. You may show a loss – unlikely after so long, but far from impossible as any dot.com investor will tell you. Now you need to pause over the calculation of indexation. Price indexation factors from 1982 to 1998 are set out in the following table. If you want to find out the indexation allowance to April 1998, you multiply by the relevant factor: so if, for example, you bought shares costing £1,000 in January 1992, the price indexation would be 0.199 so that your cost post-indexation would be £1,199.

The rule is that a loss cannot be created or increased by indexation. So if you have a loss before indexation, that is the full extent of the loss which you will be allowed, and you don't need to make the index calculation. If you show a small profit before indexation, which indexation would turn into a loss then you show zero – neither a loss nor a profit. Let's hope that you have now established a profit after indexation on your net gain.

There is one final sum before you know your liability: taper

INDEXATION FACTORS

Year	Jan	Feb	Mar	Apr	May	June	Jul	Aug	Sep	Oct	Nov	Dec
1982			1.047	1.006	0.992	0.987	0.986	0.985	0.987	0.977	0.967	0.971
1983	0.968	0.960	0.956	0.929	0.921	0.917	0.906	0.898	0.889	0.883	0.876	0.871
1984	0.872	0.865	0.859	0.834	0.828	0.823	0.825	0.808	0.804	0.793	0.788	0.789
1985	0.783	0.769	0.752	0.716	0.708	0.704	0.707	0.703	0.704	0.701	0.695	0.693
1986	0.689	0.683	0.681	0.665	0.662	0.663	0.667	0.662	0.654	0.652	0.638	0.632
1987	0.626	0.620	0.616	0.597	0.596	0.596	0.597	0.593	0.588	0.580	0.573	0.574
1988	0.574	0.568	0.562	0.537	0.531	0.525	0.524	0.507	0.500	0.485	0.478	0.474
1989	0.465	0.454	0.448	0.423	0.414	0.409	0.408	0.404	0.395	0.384	0.372	0.369
1990	0.361	0.353	0.339	0.300	0.288	0.283	0.282	0.269	0.258	0.248	0.251	0.252
1991	0.249	0.242	0.237	0.222	0.218	0.213	0.215	0.213	0.208	0.204	0.199	0.198
1992	0.199	0.193	0.189	0.171	0.167	0.167	0.171	0.171	0.166	0.162	0.164	0.168
1993	0.179	0.171	0.167	0.156	0.152	0.153	0.156	0.151	0.146	0.147	0.148	0.146
1994	0.151	0.144	0.141	0.128	0.124	0.124	0.129	0.124	0.121	0.120	0.119	0.114
1995	0.114	0.107	0.102	0.091	0.087	0.085	0.091	0.085	0.080	0.085	0.085	0.079
1996	0.083	0.078	0.073	0.066	0.063	0.063	0.067	0.062	0.057	0.057	0.057	0.053
1997	0.053	0.049	0.046	0.040	0.036	0.032	0.032	0.026	0.021	0.019	0.019	0.016
1998	0.019	0.014	0.011									

relief. This relief was introduced by the Labour government from 1998: they drew a line under the theory that inflationary gains should not be taxed and introduced a system which reduced the amount of tax the longer you held the asset. Tax on gains made on assets bought before 1998, and sold now, can be relieved both by indexation up to 1998, and then by taper relief depending on how long it is since 1998.

Calculating Taper

If you have owned an asset for more than a year after April 1998, there is a tapering scale; you get no benefit if you sell within the first two complete years of ownership but from then on there is a sliding scale, so that after 10 years only 60% of the gain is chargeable. This scale applies to non-business assets and you get the bonus of an extra year if you held the non-business shares (or other assets) in March 1998. The scale for disposals post 5 April 2002 is as follows:

Number of Complete Years Asset Owned After 5 April 1998	Non-Business Assets Percentage Chargeable	Business Assets Percentage Chargeable
1	100	50
2	100	25
3	95	25
4	90	25
5	85	25
6	80	25
7	75	25
8	70	25
9	65	25
10 years or more	60	25

When realising capital gains during the tax year, your objective is to bring the total of taxable gains, after deducting any losses realised, as near as possible below the threshold (currently £7,900 each for husband and wife). When it comes to the question of calculating how many shares in a company need to be sold from a larger holding to accomplish this, it is fiendishly complex, bringing into play both indexation and taper relief for shares owned before 1998, and you are probably best to ask your accountant to work it out for you.

On business assets, the taper relief is much more generous, so that after two years, only 25% of the gain is taxable. "Business assets" covers shares in most privately-owned trading companies which currently extends to include shares in trading companies on the Alternative Investment Market (AIM), which count as unquoted. Investments on AIM are risky, but they offer useful advantages both for inheritance tax and capital gains tax.

How Much to Pay?

If you have made taxable capital gains for the year, you have to work out how much it will cost you. If you are a higher-rate taxpayer, the answer is simple: you pay 40%. If you pay tax at standard rate or at the lower 10% then you need to calculate whether your capital gain will push you into the higher tax bracket.

Once you know how much you are going to pay, you have about 10 months before you need to write your cheque. For example, capital gains tax for the year 5 April 2003 is payable by 31 January 2004.

What Happens to Shares in Takeovers and New Issues?

If you hold a painting over a number of years, or a valuable set of china, your asset will not change. The life of a share is different: the company could have changed its name, made a rights issue and finally been taken over. You need to be able to deal with all of these possibilities.

A change of name is straightforward, but make sure that all your records are changed and you log the change of name when you come to sell. It is not unknown for you to be challenged when you come to sell share X – there being no record of your ever having acquired it!

Rights Issue

Your company may also have made a rights issue, selling shares to shareholders on a preferential basis. Assuming that you take up all of your rights, the procedure is straightforward and you record that you have bought a certain number of shares at a certain time for a certain price.

But you may not want to take up your rights, or all of them. You may not have the funds available, or you may not be keen to add to your investment in this particular company. You have two possibilities: the first is that you simply sell the rights once stock market dealings have begun. If the value of the rights you sell is very small in relation to your holding, then your proceeds should be free from any capital gains tax.

Your second possibility is to sell sufficient of your existing shares (the "old" shares) to enable you to take up the rights to the "new". In this case, the sale of the old shares follows the normal CGT rules and you will have to do the calculation to see whether this will involve you in paying tax.

Takeover

Calculating gains on a takeover is straightforward. If the offer is all-cash, you have made a disposal – though perhaps unlooked-for on your part. If the offer consists of shares, or other kinds of securities, then the new shares simply take on the acquisition cost and date of your original investment. If you have the option of cash or securities, you may well choose in the light of your CGT situation in the tax year concerned.

In takeovers which are a mixture of cash and securities, original cost has to be allocated on the basis of market value at the time of the takeover. In a demerger, cost also has to be allocated on the relevant market values.

Bed and Breakfast Up-to-date

Bed and breakfast deals (when you sell and buy back shares to establish a gain or loss) have now been restricted but there remain some possible lines of action. One is to sell the share while your spouse buys, though your sale and his/her purchase have to be separate stand-alone transactions. The second, and simpler, course is to sell a share and buy its twin. Suppose that you have a loss on a unit trust tracker fund; you sell those units, realise your loss and invest the proceeds in another tracker fund.

Coping with CGT

Capital gains tax is complicated and it will hit you at your top rate. There are a number of things you can do to reduce the impact of CGT:

❖ Use your allowance: everyone has an allowance of £7,900, so a couple now have the ability to make in excess of £15,000 a year of gains wholly free of tax. That allowance, plus the reduction in tax which can be achieved by indexation/tapering, makes CGT so much less onerous than income tax. Always remember that this allowance does not carry forward; if you do not use it during the tax year, it is lost.

❖ Wherever you can, use your annual allowance by realising shares and buying others with the same characteristics. In the example already quoted, you can sell one tracker and buy another to crystallise a loss or to use your annual allowance and uplift the cost base of your investment. Some people believe that, as they do not wish to sell, there is no need to act. But circumstances can change; uplifting the cost of your shares can be achieved at little cost in return for substantial potential benefit. That is an appealing proposition.

❖ Consider putting your assets into joint ownership or giving assets to your spouse. This has benefits for income tax; for CGT it makes sense to exploit the joint allowance. There is another advantage – on death, jointly owned assets go to the survivor without the need for probate. There is a disadvantage: if assets are transferred from one partner to another, the partner receiving the assets may be penalised if he/she has to go into local authority care.

❖ Where your assets include paintings or china as well as shares, make sure that you document all the expenses of looking after those assets – valuation, cleaning, insurance, safe-keeping and so on. Chattels, as the Inland Revenue calls them, are free of tax up to £6,000 – but a set of, say, six Queen Anne chairs would be regarded as a single chattel rather than six: this is an area where you should take specialist advice.

❖ Documentation is also important in looking after a second home, where you must distinguish between capital improvements and running costs.

❖　Where you have, or expect to have, substantial CGT bills, consider investing in a Venture Capital Trust or an Enterprise Investment Scheme. These plans defer CGT rather than reduce it, but at the end of the period there is the option of rolling forward your investment and continuing to defer your taxable gain. There is – as always – something of a risk in that when you come to pay the CGT you will be taxed at the rates prevailing at that time. Subject to that – and you may think that a fall is more likely than a rise in CGT – you will have deferred your liability even if you decide not to re-invest. In financial terms, a liability deferred is a liability reduced.

Inheritance Tax

The late Lord (Roy) Jenkins was famous for his aphorism on inheritance tax: IHT, he said, is a voluntary tax which is paid by people who distrust their heirs more than they dislike the Inland Revenue. The facts are rather different: IHT raises more than £2 billion a year from well over 20,000 estates. This is no voluntary tax, unless he meant that if you give away all of your assets then no inheritance tax will arise; that is true, but not very helpful!

Who Pays IHT?

Many, if not most, of the people reading this book will leave estates which have to pay IHT. The way it works is simple: on death your heirs pay at the rate of 40% tax on all your assets, including your house, to the extent that their value exceeds £255,000. In many cases, the house alone is worth more than that amount. Remember that you have to include all of your investments, personal effects and life assurance policies. Remember also that your assets will all be frozen, including your bank account, until the inheritance tax has been paid.

Transferring Assets

Most people will transfer, or give away, assets during their lifetime: exempt transfers are gifts which do not form part of your estate for tax purposes and therefore do not produce a liability for IHT. This is an important group and comprises:

❖ Transfers between husband and wife – assuming that both are domiciled in the UK. These transfers, whether made during your lifetime or in your will on death, are free from IHT. There is an important trap here for the unwary: if you leave all of your assets to your spouse, no IHT will arise. But leaving your entire estate in this way can build up a large IHT liability on the second death. Instead, you should leave your estate to your spouse subject to leaving the 'nil rate band' (this is the amount below which no IHT arises) to your heirs. To do this you need to make a will. You may be concerned that leaving the nil rate amount to others will impact on your spouse's living standards; later we discuss how to deal with this.

❖ Lifetime transfers of up to £3,000 a year can be made free of IHT, and this allowance can be carried forward for one year. You can also make an unlimited number of small gifts, defined as less than £250.

❖ Gifts in consideration of marriage. The parents of the bride and groom can give £5,000 and grandparents can give £2,500. Anyone else may give £1,000.

❖ Normal expenditure out of income. This is an extremely important way to mitigate IHT. These gifts should not affect your standard of living and should form part of a regular pattern of spending. This could include, for instance, premiums paid by standing order to an insurance policy which is written in trust for the benefit of your heirs. One note of caution: there are no official guidelines on how much exemption the Inland Revenue will agree.

❖ Lifetime gifts for the maintenance of dependants – this includes your spouse or former spouse and children in full-time education.

❖ Gifts to UK recognised charities are exempt, including bequests to universities and national museums. An overseas charity may not count, but many have set up UK offshoots to benefit from bequests and gift aid donations out of income.

❖ Gifts to political parties are free from IHT whether made during your lifetime or as part of your estate.

IHT on Gifts

The majority of large gifts are potentially exempt transfers which are made to individuals or to most types of trust. No IHT will be payable so long as the donor lives for at least seven years following the date of the gift. As we shall see, when deciding how to reduce the impact of IHT, you must not retain an interest in the gift or derive any continuing benefit from it: for example, if you give your holiday flat to your daughter and continue to use it, the gift will be void. This is known as a 'gift with reservation', i.e. not really a gift at all which is simply added to your estate and taxed accordingly. The second point of caution is that the gift, unless it consists of cash, may give you a bill for capital gains tax. You can give shares to your son, but you will be treated as having realised them for current market value. There is no logic in saving IHT in the future if that means paying capital gains tax now, especially as CGT is wiped out at death.

If you make a gift which is a potentially exempt transfer but die within the seven years, IHT will be charged on a tapering basis (unless your transaction falls within the annual exemption). There is no relief if you die within the first three years, but there will be a 20% reduction if you die in years 3-4, rising to 80% in years 6-7 and no IHT at all after the seventh anniversary.

Business and Agriculture Reliefs

These are valuable reliefs for people who own private businesses or agricultural property. Their rationale is that businesses ought not have to be split up or sold when one of the principals dies; the way they work is to reduce the value of the asset for IHT purposes which means that the amount of tax payable is also reduced.

There are series of rules governing these reliefs, and anyone involved should certainly take specialist advice: in agricultural property relief, there are rules governing how long the property has been owned and occupied, while in companies there are rules affecting the type of business which is carried on and the treatment of non-business assets which may be held within the company.

All that being said, the reliefs available are well worth consideration. For example, 100% reduction in value is offered in several sectors, such as:

❖ Agricultural property with vacant possession.
❖ Sole trader's business or interest in a partnership.
❖ Holdings of voting shares in a private unquoted trading company – and this currently includes qualifying shares listed on the Alternative Investment Market.

One final word on reliefs: do not forget quick succession relief, which can become important where relatives die within a few years of each other after making bequests. This relief works to reduce the tax payable on death where the estate had received assets on which IHT was paid during the previous five years. This works on the taper system, so that death within one year will see all the tax relieved, down to 20% in five years.

How to Mitigate Inheritance Tax

The first important step is to make a will; this is something which many adults in this country, amazingly, have failed to do. For a couple, both husband and wife should make wills. Where assets are owned jointly, which will probably apply to the home and shares, then these will pass to the survivor. But this does not apply to assets which are in single ownership, such as a bank account or an ISA which may not, under official regulations, be held jointly. Dying without having made a proper will (not, please, a DIY will: pay the fee and go to a solicitor) may lead to an unnecessary inheritance tax bill. More fundamentally, the assets may not go where you wanted them to: the intestacy rules will apply. In England, this means that an only child, who is not married, has no children, no uncles or aunts or first cousins and no living parents or grandparents will have his estate handed over to the Crown.

For an unmarried couple, making a will is particularly important: the surviving partner – as opposed to spouse – receives nothing under the intestacy rules and has no automatic right to act as a personal representative. For tax purposes, cohabiting couples are generally treated as unconnected individuals – which means that there are no equivalent exemptions to the freedom from CGT and IHT which applies to gifts between spouses. Most important of all, assets which pass to the surviving partner are subject to IHT at the normal rate. Common law marriages are not recognised in the UK, though there is pressure for the law to be changed.

It is important to make a will and it is also important to keep it up to date. There is, at present, a way of dealing with an out-of-date will through a deed of variation – but no-one would be surprised to see legislation to prevent this. Essentially, it is possible for the beneficiaries within two years to re-write a will, provided that every beneficiary whose inheritance is reduced agrees to it. As long as it is completed within two years of death, IHT will be charged as if the deed of variation represented the will.

A beneficiary can renounce his bequest in favour of someone else (such as his children) while the testator is still alive. This could be useful if a deed of variation cannot be arranged or if they are later prevented by legislation.

Using the 'Nil Rate' Band

One way a deed of variation can be used is the case mentioned earlier, where the will simply left all the estate to the surviving spouse. In that way, no IHT is payable – but at the cost of paying more IHT than necessary in the future, when the spouse dies. The solution is to bequeath the amount of nil rate band to the children, everything else going to the surviving spouse. On the death of the survivor, there will be a saving of 40% of the nil rate band, or £102,000 – too much to ignore.

If the will did not originally provide for this use of the nil rate band, then a deed of variation can do so instead. One point of concern is that this bequest of nil rate assets could raise problems, in that the survivor will need those assets, or at least the income from them. The solution is to bequeath investments, up to the amount of the nil rate band, to a discretionary trust which is written into the will, or the variation. This discretionary trust could have your spouse, children and grandchildren as beneficiaries so that the trustees could pay out income and/or capital to your spouse as a beneficiary under the trust. In this area you need professional help.

How to Give Away a Flat

Mitigating the impact of IHT, it will now be clear, is not a simple process. Probably the simplest way forward is to take some likely situations and see what you should and should not do. For the first case, assume that you have a holiday flat or a second home which you would like to give, say, to your daughter but which you and your wife would like to go on using. You are now in the minefield of gifts with reservation: if you simply transfer ownership of the flat (having swallowed any capital gains tax) and go on using it, you will have gone nowhere in IHT terms. You have a choice: you can stop using the flat and make sure that all bills, electoral registration, car parking, etc., etc., are transferred to your daughter. In that way, you have ceased to have an interest and derive no continuing benefit. If you wish after all to go on using the flat, then you must pay her a market rent – preferably which is supported by a local estate agent. As a refinement you could put the flat into a trust of which your daughter is a beneficiary and pay the rent to the trust. That should work, but is expensive in terms of income tax: you pay the rent out of your net income while your daughter will have to pay income tax on the rent. The conclusion must be that you either give up the flat to your daughter or leave things as they are and use one of the mitigation ideas which follow.

IHT and Your Home

For many people, their home will represent the greater part of their estate. IHT planning for one's home – your principal private residence – should be kept simple. Some highly ingenious schemes for large homes evolved during the 1990s but these were checked by legislation. Owners of large and valuable houses could consider trust schemes, but these are not free from risk; anyone attracted by exotic planning must remember that the Inland Revenue can attack schemes which they can show were set up with the principal aim of avoiding tax, not commercial logic. For many people, the rise in property values can pose an acute dilemma: their home has been brought into the IHT area, while they have only limited cash and investments. A couple in this situation face the prospect that their children, when they inherit the family home, will have to sell it in order to pay the IHT. The most practical course is for the couple to take out an insurance policy in trust for their children – the policy to pay out on the second death, as the property would pass to the survivor on the first death. As the policy is written in trust for the children, it would not form part of the estate. The policy premiums would be gifts but if the couple start the policy reasonably soon after retirement (and they enjoy average good health) the premiums should be well inside the exemption limits. If the children are prospering, they could arrange a policy and pay the premium themselves.

IHT – When Your Home is Your Principal Asset

But many people face the most difficult of dilemmas – the value of their home means it will pay IHT, but they do not have the surplus funds to take out a policy as just described. If they have sufficient income, they could re-mortgage and use the money to buy a single premium whole of life assurance which is placed in trust. The payout under the policy would be free of IHT – but the owners would have been paying mortgage interest during their lifetime.

Where it would be difficult to pay the mortgage interest out of income, the answer is equity release – probably home reversion. The owners sell part of their house to a reversionary company and use the proceeds to buy a policy in trust. This means that the house will have to be sold after both spouses have died. And home reversion plans will provide significant values only when both spouses are in their late 70s and 80s.

Tenancies in Common

Pensioners who are concerned about future IHT on their home could also ponder tenancies in common. When a husband and wife jointly own a house or a bank account, this will generally take the form of joint tenancies – they own identical equal shares and one may not sell or give away his or her part without the agreement of the other.

In England and Wales there is the alternative of tenancies in common: these represent separate interests, which need not be equal, and each spouse may sell or give his or hers away as he or she wishes. For IHT planning, a husband or wife could leave his or her share to the children or grandchildren – so that if this share comes within the tax-free band (assuming half shares, that the house is worth around £500,000), there will be no IHT to pay. Creating tenancies in common simply requires a signed joint statement; the practical point is to ensure that the surviving spouse has a secure home.

Gift and Loan Schemes

The objective of IHT mitigation, in essence, is to reduce the size of your estate without affecting your living standards. One recognised route is the gift and loan scheme – though this is best started soon after retirement. This is how it works: you take out a small investment bond and put it into trust; you then make a loan to the trustees (probably interest-free and repayable on demand) which they use to buy another bond. As at present withdrawals of up to 5% a year are free of current tax, the trustees (who include yourself) arrange for withdrawals to repay the loan, which gives you an income. Once the loan has been repaid the gift and all its growth will be outside your estate.

These schemes underline a simple but important point about making gifts: it makes best sense to give assets which will grow in value, such as insurance policies or high quality zero-coupon issues made by a leading investment group and whose quality can be independently verified. The gift is valued at the time it is made, so that the rise in value takes place outside your estate.

Taking Action

Taking action to reduce IHT sounds like hassle, which to a degree it is – though professionals nowadays are familiar with the mitigation scene. All these ideas – and there are plenty more – can essentially be reduced to four practical steps:

❖ Make a will – and make sure you use the nil rate band.
❖ Be certain that you are happy about making gifts in terms of your own financial security – and remember that some gifts will mean your paying capital gains tax.
❖ Use life assurance, probably in trust for your beneficiaries: paying premiums is a useful way of using your annual small gift exemption.

❖ Think about trusts to leave you control over gifts – with you as a trustee.

❖ Before you begin, do work out your wealth and your likely IHT liability.

Business Tax Breaks

Many of the people reading this book will have retired from business. You may have been self-employed or owned or held an interest in a small business or a farm.

You stand to benefit from a number of tax concessions, though in many cases you will need to take professional advice. Some of the points will arise in other chapters, but a round-up of business tax breaks may prove helpful.

Inheritance Tax Concessions

If you held an interest in a small business or farm, important concessions are available but you will almost certainly need advice from an accountant. For example, business relief means there will be no IHT on assets such as land, buildings and stock which form part of a trading business. There are similar wide-ranging concessions on farmland which you owned and farmed yourself or let to others to farm.

Two important classes of shares also rank for relief as business assets. One is a controlling interest in a listed company, where the value is halved for IHT calculations. Treatment of that class of share seems reasonable, but the second and lesser-known concession applies to trading companies listed on the Alternative Investment Market – AIM. Provided they have been held for at least two years, qualifying AIM shares are wholly free of inheritance tax – which may explain why some substantial companies in which the directors hold an interest remain on that market. Unquoted shares and over-the-counter securities (which may be traded through a broker but are not necessarily listed on a recognised stock exchange) are treated in the same way.

CGT Reduction

The very useful IHT concessions receive parallel treatment under capital gains tax. Relief is available when you sell your business provided you are aged over 50 or are retiring because of ill-health. And you can sell if you are over 50 without being compelled to retire. (The government has indicated it may change 50 to 55.)

CGT can also be deferred (this principle arises in Enterprise Investment Schemes and Venture Capital Trusts) if you sell a business asset and replace it by another business asset: this is known as roll-over relief. The scope of business assets is very wide – land, buildings, plant and machinery, but there were reports recently that the Revenue planned to modify CGT relief on shares or business assets given to children.

In shares, unquoted shares count as business assets and attract the lower rates of tax. Again, in AIM-listed trading companies, shares count as unquoted so that gains attract less tax than the disposal of fully listed equities. AIM shares can be risky, being often small companies, but the tax concessions on both IHT and CGT make them a useful part of overall tax efficiency.

Closing Your Business

Closing your business or your self-employment activities can be made tax-effective – but this is an area where you will need specialist advice. For example, you may find expenses arising even after you have closed the business – say legal costs because of a dispute relating to the business's activities. Some of these expenses can be charged against your income in the years when they arise, even though your business has been closed.

A more positive side of this situation is what are called post-cessation receipts, i.e. money you receive relating to your business even though you have permanently closed it. You may have been taxed on a cash basis – on the money that was actually paid into your bank. In that case, one of your customers may simply have paid you late. Alternatively, you may have been taxed on an earnings basis – in effect, on the invoices which you have issued. (From the taxpayer's standpoint, this basis means that you can pay tax on money you have not received, and may not receive for some time.) In that case, your late income will simply represent a debtor, fee or perhaps commission which for some reason was not included in your outstandings. These post-cessation receipts will be taxed under the same Schedule D rules which were used when you were still trading as self-employed.

The Final Tax Bill

The system for taxing your closing year is thankfully straightforward – the assessment is based on the actual profits from the previous 6 April until the date of cessation. There is one complication, known as 'overlap', which will arise if you originally chose an accounting date other than April 5. The aim is to ensure that you are not taxed twice, so that you can deduct overlap profits when you cease the business.

Separation and Divorce

The tax aspects, at least, of separation and divorce have been simplified over recent years:

-   The ex-spouse receiving maintenance gets the money without any deduction for tax.
-   The ex-spouse paying maintenance does not get any tax relief – with one exception. The amount of relief is small and is available only where one or other of the two ex-spouses was born before 6 April 1935. Even this relief ends if the spouse getting it re-marries, and it is available only for payments to a former spouse – not to children.

An ex-spouse who is paying maintenance does so effectively out of after-tax income. The Inland Revenue will want maintenance payments to be made on a formal basis – a letter should do.

Year of Separation

In the eyes of the Inland Revenue, an ex-spouse is a single person. In previous years, separation or divorce was acknowledged only when there was an enforceable legal agreement. The rules are less formal nowadays, but you should tell the Inland Revenue when you decide to separate and therefore change your tax status.

Capital Gains Rather Than Income

The concessions on capital gains tax for separated and divorced people mean that anyone paying maintenance should consider carefully basing payments on capital – as opposed to paying monthly maintenance out of taxed income.

During the tax year when separation takes place, transfers can still take place between the spouses without attracting any capital gains tax. An important concession is that for a further three years there will be no capital gains tax if an ex-spouse sells or gives the former family home. That should give time for the two ex-spouses to agree on a settlement. To the extent that shares are involved (especially when the spouse paying maintenance is showing capital gains) it makes sense to agree on separation during the early part of the financial year, in order to give time for the share transfers to be made effective. If the shares are showing losses, the ex-spouse will want to realise them and register a loss, transferring cash instead.

There is an oddity on inheritance tax: gifts between separated spouses are free of IHT, but once they are divorced the gifts may fall under the tax. Where significant amounts are involved under CGT and/or IHT, it will be prudent to take professional advice.

Children and Tax

Where the former married couple had a child or children under the age of 16, they would be eligible for Child Tax Credit. (See page 20.) On the assumption that the child or children will spend time with both parents, the credit can be shared between you as you agree. If you are unable to agree, then the Inland Revenue will decide.

Splitting the Pension

Probably the biggest recent change in divorce came in the 1990s, when it became possible to split pension rights. In a typical case, the pension rights built up by one spouse in a company pension scheme – personal and stakeholder plans are also covered – can now be split with the other. Before then, pension assets were not included in a divorce settlement which was widely regarded as unfair.

The most usual way of splitting is to share the capital value, but it is also possible for the spouse without a pension to join the other's scheme. Actuarial values need expert assessment; at present pension splitting is available only to married couples who divorce, not to unmarried partners who split up.

Foreign Divorce

This is a specialist area; a rough outline is as follows: where the ex-spouse paying maintenance lives in the UK, the general rules apply – no tax concessions unless one or other was aged over 65 in April 2000, and then only limited benefits. If the ex-spouse receiving maintenance lives in the UK, the position used to be that they would be liable for tax. Now, all EU countries have been placed on the same basis as the UK itself.

If the one paying maintenance wants to take advantage of the modest tax concession, then the separation should be formalised to the extent that the maintenance payments are enforceable – a letter written to the recipient should be enough – as is the case with ex-spouses both of whom live in the UK.

Reconciliation

The Inland Revenue smiles on reconciliation to the extent that a year's marriage allowance will be allowed for the tax year in which reconciliation takes place. It follows that a reconciliation which takes place on 31 March is potentially more valuable than one which occurs ten days later – with you both, in this case, telling the Inland Revenue.

Enterprise Investment Schemes

A tradition seems to have been established for governments to give tax breaks to investors if they are prepared to make some-what risky investments in small industrial businesses. The Business Expansion Scheme is a familiar memory, which was replaced in 1994 by the Enterprise Investment Scheme. As is the way with governments, the replacement is less generous and more complex. But EIS is worth consideration by pensioners, especially those paying higher rate income tax; and for pensioners nursing a large capital gain, EIS could be very attractive.

The essentials of an EIS investment are that you save income tax at 20%; you get capital gains exemption on the investment and the ability to carry back part of the relief to the previous tax year. Potentially most interesting of all is the ability to defer capital gains tax on any other asset plus the ability to roll over gains into later EIS investments. The maximum investment is set at £150,000 a year and the shares must be held for three years.

There will also be freedom from inheritance tax, provided two years have elapsed: EIS investments count as business assets – if, for example, they are AIM trading companies.

60% Off Tax!

If you invest in newly issued 'shares' of an EIS scheme, the income tax rebate is worth 20%. You could, by investing the maximum, arrange a rebate of up to £30,000. But the major appeal of your EIS investment is that it allows you to defer a bill for capital gains tax (CGT) on profits you have made from selling other assets – maybe a second home or a long-standing share portfolio – provided that you make the EIS investment between one year before and three years after the disposal which has produced your gain. In this way, you have an income tax saving of 20% plus a CGT deferment at your marginal rate up to 40%; you have achieved a 60% tax reduction!

On the EIS shares themselves, you can sell these free of CGT once you have held them for the minimum three years. If you are unfortunate enough to make a loss on your EIS investment, you can arrange to have this loss set against your income. In financial terms, you are gaining through an income tax rebate and a CGT deferment: remember that a liability deferred is a liability reduced. You are regarded as having re-invested your capital gain in the EIS shares and your gain will be taxed only when you eventually sell the shares. When that time comes, you will still have the option of reinvesting in another EIS company.

Which Companies Qualify?

Behind all this interesting arithmetic is the fundamental assumption that you choose a successful investment – or at the very least one that does not fail. The range of qualifying companies is broadly similar to the former Business Expansion Scheme: companies whose income comes mainly from royalties and licences, for example, will not qualify except for film production and distribution. The essence of qualification is that the company should be an unquoted trading business, though in this case unquoted includes qualifying companies on the

Alternative Investment Market. One difference from BES is that private rented housing does not qualify.

You should be aware also of the traditional Inland Revenue provisions: the company must be managed on a commercial basis with a view to profit throughout the period which begins with the issue of EIS-eligible shares. EIS relief will not be forthcoming if the issue forms part of a scheme whose main purpose is to avoid tax – with the Inland Revenue deciding! What happens in practice is that the directors will approach the Inland Revenue and ask for provisional confirmation that the company qualifies; if you are investing, you should look for this statement. Once the company is up and trading, the directors will send certificates to their investors enabling them to claim tax relief.

One issue is that the tax authorities may revoke the EIS clearance. This is not common, but nor is it unknown, so that it makes sense to establish either direct or through your adviser that a particular scheme has been cleared at the right, appropriately senior, official level.

Capital Gains Tax Relief: The Detail

For many people, this relief will represent the most appealing part of EIS. You can defer the tax arising from a capital gain on any asset provided the EIS shares are bought between one year before and three years after the disposal. The relief is not automatic and you have to make a claim to the Inland Revenue.

One good piece of news is the carry-back provisions. Under the EIS rules, half of what you invest during the first part of the financial year, that is between 6 April and 5 October, can be carried back to the previous tax year; there is a limit of £25,000 on the amount of the carry-back. If you make a loss on your EIS shares, it can be set against other capital gains or – by election – against income.

Who is Eligible?

One thing you cannot do (which would otherwise be a frequent way of investing in a private or AIM-listed company) is to buy shares from the founder. In that case you would not get EIS relief. The EIS shares have to be new shares issued by the company. There are further limits on the amount a company can raise and on the size of the company itself.

Who Can Invest?

Just as eligible companies are hedged round with official qualifications, so are the people who can buy shares and claim EIS relief. This is especially important for investors who often are attracted to invest in a private business because they know the company and the people, and often because they have played some part in the company's development.

Rather surprisingly, you do not have to be a UK resident, though EIS relief is available only against UK taxable income. (By the same logic, the company itself does not have to be resident in the UK, but its operations must be located here.)

Qualifying Investor

The first qualification for being a qualifying investor – that is, being able to claim EIS relief – is that you must not have been connected with the company during the previous two years. Nor may you become connected within five years after the issue of the shares. Connection is fairly widely drawn: neither you nor your associates (spouse, family or partner) may be an employee, partner or paid director of the company. Nor may you hold more than 30% of the shares nor have rights over 30% of the assets. There is one exception: you may become a paid director and qualify for EIS relief provided you were not connected with the company before the shares were issued. One useful rule is that applications from joint investors are allowed, in which case the tax reliefs are apportioned equally.

EIS to Defer Capital Gains Tax

EIS rules have been relaxed significantly over the years. The maximum that may be invested has been increased and the number of years for which shares must be held has been reduced. (One suspects that these concessions were made because demand was held back by the lack of contracted exit schemes.)

The principal attraction of EIS schemes lies in the deferral of capital gains tax: the income tax concession is useful but in itself

is hardly adequate compensation for the inherent risks of buying shares in small companies. For people with large unrealised
capital gains, the appeal lies in the ability to defer or roll over
the payment of CGT until later.

Venture Capital Trusts

Venture Capital Trusts represent in effect the investment trust
equivalent of EIS investment. Since they were introduced, a year
after the EIS scheme, VCTs have attracted around £1 billion of
investors' funds – also as part of the government's aim to
channel funds into the small and medium company sector.

VCT shares are quoted, which represents an obvious advantage for re-sale, but the risk of buying into small companies
remains. Because of the investment trust structure, there are few
rules for investors – unlike EIS – but quite elaborate guidelines
on how VCTs may operate: to begin with, they need Inland
Revenue approval, which can be provisional. As with EIS, the
shares must be newly issued: the tax advantages are restricted to
the cost of subscribing for eligible shares issued by a qualifying
company. The scheme has no application to shares bought from
a previous owner – only the cost of subscribing for shares issued
by a company can obtain relief.

Rules for Investors

For someone who wants to buy into VCT, the only test is that you
have to be at least 18 years old. As with the EIS, you get 20% tax
relief on the amount you invest in a VCT but the maximum is less:
£100,000 in a tax year. You now have to hold the shares for three
years. All the other tax advantages apply: dividends from a VCT
come tax free. Any gain you make on your VCT investment is also
free of tax but by the same token losses cannot be set against gains
made elsewhere. Most important is that all of your investment
can be used to defer a capital gain. In this case (more rigorous than
EIS) the gains must arise during the year before and the year after
the VCT shares are issued. The relief will end once you sell your
VCT shares, unless you replace them with others.

What a VCT Can Do

Behind the different official rules for EIS and VCTs seems to lie
the view that a spread of investments, where the parent entity

is listed, will be less risky. This may prove to be true, but there is also a cost in the VCT investment trust-type organisation. Typically costs are 5% on issue with running costs of about 3.5% a year and probably some sort of management incentive.

The wide-ranging rules for a VCT begin by stating that it must invest 80% of its fund within a year. At least 70% of the total fund must be invested in unquoted companies which trade mainly in the UK – though the Alternative Investment Market (AIM) is again counted as unquoted. At least 30% of the VCT's investments must be in ordinary shares: the holding in any one company must not exceed 15% of its investments nor may it retain more than 15% of its income from shares. (These very detailed rules are intended, one supposes, to follow the rules for listed investment trusts.) The kind of company it can invest in is very similar to the EIS list – licensing and royalty-based businesses are excluded as are many asset-backed companies, such as property development, farming, hotels and nursing homes.

There is a final set of rules which are meant to keep VCTs investing in small and medium companies, and these again shadow the EIS rules. Investments of no more than £1 million in any one company count towards the 70% target but not if the company's gross assets exceed the £15-16 million level specified in the EIS legislation.

Dividend Prospects

An investor who has puzzled his way through the VCT rules will realise that up to 30% of assets can be held in gilt-edged or other income-producing investments. This is a useful source from which dividends can be paid. A second source for possible dividends is that investments in the underlying companies may include debt issues or preference shares. Thirdly, capital gains released within the VCT may also be capable of being distributed as dividends. Some of the most popular VCTs have focused on AIM where ordinary shares generally offer a modest yield.

How Appealing are VCTs?

Your first step is to look at performance. One suspects that this will be easier in a few years' time. So far, an analysis of around 70 VCTs shows no clear pattern. Some have easily out-performed the market as a whole, while some have done worse. Nor does there yet seem to be any clear lead for a particular management group. So far as one can generalise, AIM-based VCTs seem to have performed better with less volatility. Until now, the market in VCT shares has tended to be thin, not least because any investor selling within the early years would lose his potentially valuable tax benefits. One of the key questions, once a market in VCT shares has been well established, is what level of discount to net assets will emerge. Traditional investment trusts usually stand at a discount to underlying assets, with the size of the discount tending to vary with the general level of the market. You can argue it both ways. Because they invest in small and medium unlisted companies, which are risky, VCTs should stand at a larger discount. But because their growth possibilities are greater than typical equities, some people will feel that the discount should be smaller!

Buying VCT Shares

Investing in a VCT can be uncertain, like buying any other type of newly issued share. VCTs tend to be sold in the last quarter of the financial year and sponsors normally set minimum levels of support. Whether these levels are reached depends partly on investment sentiment at the time; in the early part of 2002, for example, sentiment was uncertain so that the level of VCT investment was around half that of the previous year and some sponsors withdrew their funds. This could be important for an investor who wanted to buy into a VCT in order to satisfy a particular capital gains tax problem. The only answer for a would-be VCT investor is to invest early and split your investment between at least two trusts. And one important judgment lies in the record and standing of the management group itself – an assessment which is made easier because several of the sponsors manage related investments, in unit trusts and elsewhere.

Buy or Wait?

Judging how the VCT market will develop as it matures is the vital question. Overall market sentiment and the level of equities as a whole will be important. Also important will be the kind of return earned by the £1 billion or so which went into VCTs after they were created in the mid-1990s. AIM-oriented VCTs have done well and become popular with investors, but even here the longer term prospects for AIM itself are not entirely clear. But for an investor with a capital gains tax liability, the VCT appeal of a 20% cashback and a 40% deferment represent a powerful combination.

Chapter 2:

Savings and Investment

Investment Strategy

For your savings, you need an investment portfolio that will perform over a 20-year-(or more) life. For most people, this will mean holding stocks and shares. But which and how much? There is an old Wall Street motto which has stood the test of time: take your age from 100, you then have the percentage of your savings which should be in equities.

Equities and How to Manage Them

The long-term case for equities, or ordinary shares, is familiar but it remains important especially in the context of a 20-year view. This needs repeating after the bruising experiences of recent years. The case is this: between 1969 and 2000, shares produced positive returns in 75% of the one-year periods and negative returns in 25%. But if you look at five-year periods the balance changes to 89% positive and 11% negative; if you look at 10-year periods the negative returns disappear. This means that, over those years, anyone able to take a five-year view of equities was very likely to come out ahead; anyone able to take a 10-year view was certain to come out ahead.

We are all aware that the future may not resemble the past, but the past is all that we can know. With that qualification, here is the 100-year story:

Average Annual Real Return 1899-1999 (% a year)

Deposit	1.6
Fixed Interest	1.0
Equities	5.7

(Source: Barclays Capital)

57

You might think, with these numbers, that you should put all your money into equities. The reason for the Wall Street motto is partly risk (don't put all your eggs in one basket), partly ignorance (the future may not be like the past), partly the shorter time horizon for an older person compared with a 40-year-old, and the greater importance of income once you have retired.

You may want to make your own investment decisions. It will help if you have some knowledge of procedures; of fundamental importance is that you regularly set aside some time – maybe just a quarter of an hour every week – to review your investments. Alternatively, you may seek help from a stockbroker. He will offer advisory or discretionary service – probably the latter. If he is advisory, he will make suggestions but take no action without your prior agreement. If he has a discretionary mandate, he will be free to act within the guidelines which have been agreed with you, and you will be told what deals he has carried out. Probably he will send you copies of contract notes.

Self Help

Whichever route you choose for managing your portfolio, it makes sense for you to build up some knowledge. The financial press is wide-ranging, especially at weekends, and financial information comes over readily on the internet. It must be sensible for you to be able to hold a dialogue with someone who is managing your portfolio. One hopes that the process of protecting and improving your wealth will actually be fun! And there are aspects to your portfolio which may raise sensitive issues: it could make sense, as discussed in Chapter 1, to move some shares into joint names or even transfer them outright to the spouse with the lower tax rate.

Choosing individual shares is the most difficult, and the most rewarding of investment activities. There is a great deal in the press, in circulars from brokers and advisers and organisations which specialise in investment advice. Use your own judgment, when you assess a shop, a garage or even a restaurant! There is one caveat: what you are buying is a share, but what you are assessing is a company. Company X may be large and well-run, but its shares may have gone ahead and be expensive. Company Y may be performing badly, but its shares may have been over-sold or rivals may be contemplating a takeover bid; in either of these situations, Y's shares will be worth buying.

Life After Mr Sandler

Over the next few years, if the Sandler proposals of mid-2002 (previously referred to on page 18) are enacted, a new range of investment products will be created, following the model of stakeholder pensions. These products would have no initial charges, a cap on annual charges probably of 1% and no exit penalties. Alongside pensions, these new stakeholder schemes would include unit trusts and insurance products.

Retired men and women, like everyone else, will have to wait for the detail. But three cautionary points need to be made:

1. Stakeholder pensions offer a significant tax break to those under 75. As the section on stakeholder pensions shows, you can buy £100 worth of pension for £78. That prospect has a clear appeal: what will be the incentives for the new products?
2. Some government ministers called these new products "safe havens" – a clear case of mis-selling. If the unit trusts were trackers, then they would fall along with stock markets as in 2000, 2001 and 2002.
3. These products will be sold as packages by distributors – with minimum regulation. The buyer will have to decide whether the package is right for him, and there will be no come-back for mis-selling.

You must compare these products with what can be bought in the market place. Take tracker unit trusts: you can already buy UK trackers for no initial charge, no exit charge and an annual management fee of 0.3%. If the new products do better, that would be impressive indeed; let's wait and see.

Building a Portfolio

You may want to choose your own shares, as do many people, as opposed to paying a unit or investment trust manager. If your share selection is sound – or if you are just lucky – then your portfolio may perform well.

There are many ways to build a share portfolio. Here is one typical method: you divide your shares into 40% blue chips, 40% defensive shares and 20% higher risk.

BLUE CHIPS V UTILITIES

Your first 40% of blue chips should come from the top companies in the index. These are the UK's major corporations, in oil, pharmaceuticals, banking and retailing. These shares can be volatile, as buyers of telecoms will know. Each industry has its own risks: the oil price, and therefore profits, can be affected by world politics; a pharmaceutical company will be boosted if its drug is approved in the US – or the opposite.

Your next 40% should be defensive shares which will be less affected by changes in the overall economy. They will offer less exciting growth prospects than the blue chips but they often offer higher dividend yields. This covers a wide range, notably the utilities, along with shares in food, drink and tobacco. These shares are not free from risk but they are in general lower risk than blue chips – hence the higher return.

YOUR LAST 20%

This section is for you to indulge your tastes – realising that you may make mistakes, but that if you spread your holdings you should not lose all. Some people buy shares in companies they deal with – say retailers – which they find impressive. Another way to invest this 20% is to choose several – not just one or two – "penny" shares. These are low-priced shares, often in companies which are having problems, where the appeal lies in the prospect of doubling your money! But you may lose most if not all.

There are two basic rules. First, make sure that you have a spread of interests – not just in terms of industry, but in overseas countries. You may prefer not to buy US or European shares direct, but the UK companies in which you invest should trade in those areas. Secondly, keep yourself informed: you should look at the internet or the business section of a newspaper every day, ideally, or at a minimum once a week.

Unit Trusts

Choosing specific shares is suitable for larger portfolios where the investor has enough wealth to spread the risk, and maybe particular knowledge or a connection. Otherwise, people look to unit trusts, or mutual funds: these are essentially pooled investment vehicles operated by a fund management group which provides full-time professional guidance. (Many have now become OEICs, open-ended investment companies; the differences are mainly technical.)

There is now a very wide range of unit trusts based on equities: growth trusts, those offering above-average income, trusts specialising in particular sectors and in specific countries. Essential details of leading unit trusts appear daily in the press – including the cost of management, which can be 5% initially plus 1% a year or more.

'Tracker' unit trusts (see overleaf) are designed so that their value rises or falls in proportion with the chosen stock market index, e.g. the FTSE 100. Charges on these are usually much lower.

You can buy units direct by contacting the management group, but many people buy unit trusts through a discount broker, who will refund some or all of the initial charge (through extra units or a cash refund) and may even be prepared to hand back part of the periodic loyalty bonus he receives. Unit trusts necessarily reflect the value of the underlying shares and they are also subject to the ups and downs of commercial life – successful managers may leave, fund management companies may merge.

Investment Trusts

Investment trusts were the financial discovery of the nineteenth century: they are listed companies which buy shares in other companies. There are now more than 300, some aiming at general investment, others at specific areas. By contrast with unit trusts, they can borrow and they are permitted to plough back up to 15% of their annual income. Shares in investment trusts do not always reflect the value of the underlying assets, as unit trusts do. Investment trust shares are affected by the market and stand at varying discounts (occasionally premiums) to the value of the underlying assets.

Investment trusts appeal because their charges tend to be low and they perform well if the managers make the right gearing decisions. A recent trend has been the growth of the split trust –

capital shares which get all the growth but no income, and income shares which get all the income and no capital growth, with a fixed winding-up date for the trust. Some of these splits did badly in the difficult market conditions post-2000; you need to look carefully, or take advice, before investing; some splits borrowed from the banks and bought shares issued by other splits (the 'magic circle'). Some splits offer attractive value – but take care. In the worst case, most if not all of shareholders' funds can be lost.

Tracker Funds

The tracker is the latest and possibly the most important development in the world of unit trusts: a tracker holds a portfolio which reflects a particular stock market index, either by holding the shares in that index or by running a matched computer program. Choosing shares by computer has the immediate effect of cutting costs: you can now buy a tracker of the London market which makes no initial charge and whose annual charge is no more than 0.3%. (There are some which charge more: you need to check before you buy.)

This cost saving is significant compared with actively managed funds – especially at a time of low inflation and low performance figures. But there is a second, more fundamental, appeal of the tracker funds: research shows that only a minority of actively managed funds manage to out-perform the indices – which the trackers accurately reflect. Over a period, evidence suggests that about 20% of the actively managed funds out-perform the indices – but this may not always be the same 20%!

Trackers now offer a wide range of choice: in the UK, you can buy a tracker for the all-share index, or for the top 100 companies. And trackers now cover the US, European, Japanese and other regional markets. For investors who wish to invest in equities, the tracker has become an important tool.

Hedge Funds

Hedge funds, which receive a good deal of press coverage, are for more sophisticated investors with good nerves. (They are not advertised and you will not receive any mail shots.) A tracker fund moves in line with its index – when the market falls, it will fall. An actively managed fund may out-perform the index, but when the market falls it is of limited consolation to be told that your fund has fallen "only" by 10% when the market dropped 15%.

Hedge funds aim to make money in all market conditions – and they may look beyond shares to deal in commodities or currencies. When markets are falling, a hedge fund manager may sell short – he will sell shares which he does not own, aiming to buy them back more cheaply as prices fall. Recent history in the US tends to suggest that hedge funds have a higher risk exposure than traditional unit trusts – and there have been some spectacular problems when hedge funds borrowed heavily or made strategic mistakes. There is also the suggestion that hedge funds perform better when markets are falling.

Hedge funds can be risky, and their charges are higher than unit trusts. But they have an appeal to larger and more skilled investors. Recently, the Financial Services Authority decided not, for the present, to grant hedge fund managers greater freedom to promote their products to small savers.

Fixed Interest Funds

So far, the discussion has centred on equities – whether, and how, to buy individual shares or unit trusts. Similar thinking applies to fixed interest securities, which – from the Wall Street dictum – will form the greater part of retired people's investments. The first group of fixed interest securities is the government's own issues, or gilt-edged. These need some detailed analysis – see page 65; gilts carry a government guarantee, but the present range is of limited appeal.

Industrial Bonds

It is possible to buy bonds, or debt, issued by a particular company, in the same way as investors buy part of a gilt issue, but the market is rather specialised. There is the advantage that you have a specific repayment date but the great drawback is risk: you are putting your eggs in one basket, which is not often a good thing to do, and the blue chip of today could become the dog of tomorrow. A major company may not collapse, like an

Enron, but its bonds will be downgraded if its performance starts to falter; a downgrading by the leading debt agencies, such as Standard and Poor, and Moody's, will mean that yields rise and capital values fall.

This is why bond funds have become so popular (and for retired people, they fit especially well into an ISA) offering yields well above the banks and building societies. They spread the risk among many different companies. The ideal time to go into bond funds is when yields generally are low and falling: it is not appealing to buy a bond fund if you think that rates will rise, as this will simply lead to lower capital values.

Zero Preferences

Bond funds will represent a major fixed interest outlet for most people, but there are at least two other more exotic fixed interest stocks which are worth pondering. First of these are zero preference shares, issued mainly by investment trusts. The theory of the zero preference is simple: it offers no dividends, but instead a fixed repayment price and date, generally within the next ten years. From that information, a book of compound interest tables will give the yield. For individuals in the UK, there is a further advantage that the gain on redemption (or on sale before redemption) ranks as a capital gain: by managing your annual tax-free allowance (double for a couple), it is possible to take the gain on a zero preference (i.e. the effective yield) free of tax.

The falling markets of 2000-2002 badly affected zero preferences: some trusts suspended their listing and several went into receivership. Zero preferences rank ahead of ordinary shares, but in some cases assets fell short of total shareholders' funds. Anyone buying zero preferences now (for the tax appeal remains) should stick to major financial groups and would be well advised to seek informed opinion. Zero-coupon bonds are low risk, but these tend to be issued in the US, either by corporations or the American government.

There are two tests for zero preferences: one is cover, i.e. the amount of assets which are available to cover the payback obligation. The second test is the hurdle rate, which is the rate at which the trust assets must grow in order to meet repayment. A strong zero will show a negative hurdle rate, which means that trust assets could decline and still leave sufficient to cover the zero preference.

Look at the yield figures: as so often, a high yield can mean a high risk.

Roll-up Funds

The roll-up fund is another useful investment tool: these funds are not well-known for they are based overseas, often in the Channel Islands, so that they may not be advertised in the UK. The roll-up does not pay out any income; what it earns is ploughed back into the assets, so that the value of the shares or units grows, slightly, from day to day. Because the roll-up does not pay out, its shareholders pay no tax and can watch their units grow in value – roll-ups typically invest in high-quality deposits or short-term securities.

For a UK investor, income tax has to be paid when the units are cashed in; the taxable amount is the surplus over original cost. Part of the appeal of these funds lies in the deferment of tax and the compounding of interest on interest. But they are also useful for taxpayers who move down tax bands on retirement. You can buy roll-up funds when you are working and paying 40% tax, and then redeem them when you have retired and pay standard rate tax.

Roll-ups are also a useful way of getting exposure to foreign currency. Most of the roll-up funds offer investors a range of currencies and the ability to switch among them at no or nominal cost: you will get the rate of interest which is applicable to the particular currency. And roll-ups have appeal for expatriates – Britishers working abroad who can invest in sterling securities, at sterling rates without the hassle of the on-shore tax system.

Gilt-edged – The Government's Own Issue

Gilts – gilt-edged or government securities – are the safest investment you can buy, in the sense that security is good. Many investors have lost capital on gilts: capital values fall as interest rates rise and on most gilts there is no protection against inflation. Gilts are bonds issued by the government in respect of money it has borrowed, with fixed rates of interest, fixed dates for the payment of interest and a fixed date for repayment, or maturity. The greater part are divided into three categories – short, with a life of up to five years; medium, with a life of up to 15 years; and long, which go beyond that. There are two smaller, but useful groups – undated gilts (such as War Loan), which carry no fixed redemption date and index-linked, which are tied to the retail price index. (A note on terminology: a gilt may be quoted say 2005-10. This means that the government must redeem it by 2010 and has the power to redeem it after 2005. If the gilt is quoted 2005 onwards, there is no fixed redemption date – it is undated; the government can redeem the stock any time after 2005 – if it wishes to, or it may not. Redemption is entirely at the government's wish.)

Income v Capital

Not all that many years ago, gilts formed an essential part of everyone's investment portfolio – but times have changed. Investors moved to equities, and when they wanted fixed interest they chose bonds issued by major companies; these offered higher yields than gilts without any significant increase in risk (with one or two major exceptions!). Gilts have one great advantage, that any profits you make from selling or giving them to beneficiaries are free from gains tax – which also means that any losses you make are not allowed.

The problem for private investors for many years has been that the government has not had to issue gilts because it has been relying on budget surpluses – though for the next few years this may change, with an extra £7bn indicated for 2003-4. As a result, the structure of the gilt market has become out-of-date. At the time of writing, there are no low-coupon gilts standing at a discount to their redemption price and so appealing to higher rate taxpayers. And there are few gilts which are attractive for income, offering a yield to fit current market conditions and standing just below their redemption price. Most gilts stand well above their redemption price, which virtually guarantees erosion of capital, certainly so if you hold them until maturity.

Gilt Yields

Gilts pay interest twice a year, on specified dates – so that by choosing your stocks you can arrange to receive gilt income every quarter or even every month. The yield on gilts is the ratio of interest to capital cost, but the calculations are somewhat complex. You start with the current or running yield. Gilts are traded in units of £100, so a 6% gilt, for example, will yield income of £6 per year. If the price of the gilt has risen above £100, say to £120, for example, then you need to spend £120 in order to get your income of £6, so we say that the running yield is 5% (6% on £120 = 5%).

But you have to take into account the profit or loss which you will make on redemption on the assumption that you hold the gilt to maturity. A profit on redemption will give you a higher yield (and remember that this profit is tax-free). But if the stock which you bought for 120 is to be redeemed at 100 you will make a loss and the redemption yield will be lower.

This difference between running and redemption yields is important when assessing any fixed interest investment – see the section on bonds. If the redemption yield is higher than the running yield, you know that some securities have been bought below their redemption values. Conversely, if the redemption yield is lower than the running yield – as shown by some bond funds – you know that there will be a loss on redemption; the attractive-looking yield is being bought partly out of capital.

Buying and Selling Gilts

One of the long-standing attractions of gilts has been the operation of an effective market and the low cost of buying and selling. You can buy and sell gilts through a stockbroker, where the commission rates are lower than for ordinary shares, but for most transactions it will be cheaper to use the postal service which is provided by the Bank of England: this replaces the old Post Office register. The drawback is the one facing any postal service – that the price may move against you before the transaction is completed, while you are out of your money in the interim.

Are Gilts for You?

The appeal of gilts, as with any security, rests on price and yield. Buying a gilt is like buying a low-risk industrial bond: few individuals buy bonds, preferring the spread of risk which is given by bond funds – and as has been said, the products offered by the gilt market are at present of limited appeal.

If the absence of risk appeals to you, it could be worth thinking about one of the specialist gilt funds. These exploit the tax-free status of capital gains on gilts and aim to smooth out the interest rate risk: rates can, and sometimes do, move out of alignment, with short rates high in relation to medium and longs or vice versa.

It is difficult for individuals to take advantage of these short-term anomalies in the market. This type of arbitrage is carried out by funds and the large holders of gilts. But because the commissions on gilts are low and the rates have become slender, there is only a limited number of gilt funds available; your best sources of information are the internet and weekend press.

Corporation Stocks and PIBS

There are possible compromises between the (virtually) risk-free status of gilts and the industrial bond market. One is local authorities which raise loans through the market (though few in recent years) and advertise for deposits. These investments do not carry a government guarantee, but most people believe that Westminster would not be willing to let a local authority collapse.

One other major alternative to gilts is Permanent Interest Bearing Shares, issued by current and former building societies. These tend to offer higher yields than gilts, and the name sums up their unusual features: they are shares with no fixed redemption date, which have to be bought and sold through a stockbroker.

The capital value of PIBS is largely determined by current interest rates and by people's expectations of the short-term future. Always compare rates carefully before you buy a fixed interest investment: at one time, PIBS prices were pushed up because people saw them as a way of benefiting from building society de-mutualisation.

National Savings

National savings are big business. About half of the entire population hold some form of National Savings, equal to around £1,000 for every man, woman and child in the country. And National Savings are still growing, as people go to the post office or direct to National Savings & Investments.

Some NS products have appeal for retired people but a number do not. The size and growth of NS seem to arise from a liking for simplicity and security and the late Harold Macmillan's introduction of premium bonds – though premium bonds have been losing their interest more recently.

Premium Bonds

Premium bonds rank for prizes every month and can always be redeemed at face value – your capital is safe, at least in money terms. Premium bonds currently pay out at an average yield of 2.25% a year – a lower rate than in the past. This payout is made in prizes, which are tax-free, ranging from £50 up to £1 million. When you buy premium bonds, you are making a limited gamble with the interest on your money.

You can invest up to a maximum of £20,000 in premium bonds and people tend to buy in one of two different ways. One way is to buy a small stake, say £100, where the loss of interest is negligible and there is a chance – maybe remote – of winning a prize, even the top £1 million. The opposite policy, for the better off, is to buy the maximum and treat premium bonds as an investment.

How do Premium Bonds Compare?

The 2.25% rate for the prize fund equals 2.88% to a standard rate taxpayer and 3.75% to a higher rate taxpayer – somewhat less than you would get from a bank or building society. You may win a prize, but the odds have become very long: each holder of a £1 bond has one chance in 28,000 of winning a monthly prize. The odds on becoming a millionaire are about one in 17 billion. (Just under 90% of the total prize money is paid out in smaller prizes of £50 or £100.)

Even if you buy the maximum £20,000 of premium bonds you have rather better than a one-in-two chance of winning a prize in any one month – if you enjoy average luck. Some holders of the maximum have reported going for months without a prize; that, says the NS&I, is the luck of the draw.

Suppose that you have average luck: as a holder of £20,000 of bonds, you will receive eight or nine prizes over the year which will be probably £50 each. That represents a return of 2% tax-free which is below deposit levels. You have to value the chance of winning the top £1 million, which some lucky person has done every month since the early 1990s.

Premium Bond Administration

Administration is straightforward. Some newspapers publish the winning numbers for larger prizes; there is no need to claim any prize, which will be sent to you. Always remember to write to National Savings (this applies to all products) if you change your address: there is no point in adding to the 300,000 or so unclaimed prizes. Many people assume that, on death, the value of the premium bonds is added to the holder's estate. What in fact takes place is that the bonds remain eligible for each monthly drawing for up to 12 months after the date of death; any prizes go to the estate. After 12 months, the value of the bonds is paid into the estate. (The executors will have the option of cashing in at an earlier date.)

Other Tax-free Products

The premium bond, with its lottery-type working, has stood apart from other savings products – and has sold itself, for National Savings do not pay any commission to intermediaries. The other tax-free products are the two certificates (fixed interest and index-linked), a cash mini ISA and a TESSA ISA (only available for capital from a maturing TESSA) and children's bonus bonds. In addition to being tax-free, these products do not have to be included in your tax return or reported to the Inland Revenue.

Anyone thinking of buying into the last three products – the two ISAs and the children's bonus bonds – should compare what is available in the market. One has to say that only rarely have these three national savings products offered appealing rates. Put another way, any investor would be paying a significant premium for the backing of Government – as opposed to a major bank or financial institution – which to many people would not seem to be worthwhile.

National Savings Certificates

The two sorts of certificates, by contrast, do offer possibilities for retired people. On the fixed interest certificate, which is available two-year or five-year, with interest on maturity, the crucial judgment is to compare rates with competitors – with the appeal likely to be to retired people who are paying higher-rate tax. As a generalisation, the National Savings organisation tends to be a little slower than the market in changing rates, so fixed interest certificates may be more attractive in relative terms when rates as a whole are coming down. The reverse, alas, applies when rates are rising.

Index-linked certificates represent an entirely different perspective: also available in two- or five-year types, they pay on maturity a small premium over inflation. Their appeal is that they are tax-free and certain to beat inflation which must be the aim of all investments, but which many failed to achieve in the difficult years of 2000-2002. Index-linked certificates have a place if one believes that inflation will start to rise: because people expected a low rate of inflation in 2000-2, sales of these certificates tended to lag.

On both certificates, always watch for extension rates which are normally poor. It is hardly ever a good idea to hold certificates after maturity; they should be rolled into new certificates or cashed in. Maximum holding is £10,000 for each issue.

National Savings' Taxable Products

Half a dozen taxable (or part-taxable) products are offered: income bonds and pensioners' bonds for the over 60s; fixed rate savings bonds and capital bonds and an investment account plus an ordinary account. Here again, the test is to compare what National Savings offers with the market place – which can be found in the press at weekends and on several sites on the internet. As a generalisation, the rates in this sector offered by National Savings have tended to lag slightly behind the market, with pensioners' bonds closest though the minimum investment period is one year. Funds can be extracted early, but this will mean an interest penalty; there is not great scope in National Savings for penalty-free easy access which is readily available in the private sector. Interest is paid gross, which in theory is an advantage for people who do not pay tax but a bank will now do the same if you complete a simple form. To their credit, National Savings have greatly simplified the methods of investing which can be done using a debit card over the telephone; application forms are available over the internet.

Guaranteed Equity Bond

National Savings now has become an innovative organisation; one recent product, the Guaranteed Equity Bond, links investment to the stock market. In brief, this is a five-year bond which offers up to 65% if the stock market rises that much plus the return of your original investment. This 65% return is taxable as income when it is repaid, so for a higher rate taxpayer the maximum potential yield falls to 39%; and while your original capital is repaid, you do not receive any dividends or interest in the interim. (The guarantee therefore relates both to your principal and any repayment.) Buyers are told that they should invest only if they can leave their money untouched for the full five years. While this represents an interesting departure for National Savings – and the maximum investment, as with a number of National Savings products, is set on the high side at £1 million – you should be able to do better in competing products. Given that retired people will probably have less than half their investments in equities, and a five-year lock-up will seem restrictive to many – there are a number of better ways of achieving what this bond projects.

National Savings: A Summary

Everyone should have some premium bonds – even £100 worth just for that outside chance of a £1 million windfall. For higher rate taxpayers who can afford the outlay, the maximum holding of £20,000 may appeal: there is no gamble with your money capital, and a limited one with interest.

Fixed rate certificates will appeal almost wholly to higher rate taxpayers; from time to time they can be appealing but it is important to check corresponding market rates before buying. Index-linked certificates guarantee a yield – admittedly a small one – after tax and inflation, which must be the aim of every investor. Whether these certificates will appeal must depend on your view of future inflation; over the last few years inflation has dropped and stayed low – but times may change, especially as many retired people will think who recall the late 1970s and early 1980s.

National Savings' other tax-free and taxable products seem of limited interest, unless they meet a specific requirement. At most times and in most areas you can do better in the private sector; the extra risk is academic and the returns are often significantly better.

ISAs – The Only Tax-free Plan

The Individual Savings Account, or ISA, is the one tax-free account offered by the government into which people can place any of a wide range of investments. An ISA is not an account in its own right, but a plan or "wrapper" within which people can hold cash, insurance or stocks and shares. Anyone who is retired and pays tax should consider an ISA; if he pays higher rate tax, then he should look particularly carefully.

How ISAs Work

The rules governing ISAs are moderately complex but the advantages are so great that they are worth examination. Investors must be 18 and resident in the UK – though for a Mini cash ISA the minimum is 16. In each tax year, from 6 April to 5 April the following year, you can invest up to £7,000 in one Maxi ISA or three Mini ISAs. Note: you cannot open both a Maxi and a Mini ISA in the same tax year. Husbands and wives each have their own ISA allowance, so that a couple can invest up to £14,000 in one tax year. The allowance is not carried forward. If you don't use it, you lose it.

In a Maxi ISA, you can invest up to £7,000 with one supplier – or provider, in the jargon. You can invest the whole £7,000 in stocks and shares; alternatively, you can invest up to £3,000 in cash and up to £1,000 in life assurance, with the remainder in stocks and shares. In a Mini ISA, you can invest your £7,000 with up to three providers; the investment levels are the same – £3,000 in cash, £3,000 in stocks and shares and £1,000 in life assurance. One of the sensible proposals in the Sandler report of mid-2002 was to remove the Mini ISA limit for the cash and insurance sectors, and give investors the same £7,000 annual allowance as applies to Maxi ISAs.

TESSA-only ISAs

For completeness, and because many people hold a TESSA (an earlier tax-free savings scheme), these represent the one exception to the rules on annual allowances. Special ISAs operate for savers with TESSAs which mature. Once your TESSA matures, you can roll the capital into a TESSA-only ISA without in any way affecting your ISA allowances. But only the capital can be transferred in this way, i.e. the amount you originally invested of up to £9,000. You cannot transfer the interest which your investment has earned.

What to Buy

The fundamental appeal of an ISA is that it is free of all tax: even if you simply move £3,000 from the bank to a cash Mini ISA, you are changing from the taxable to the tax-free world.

Withdrawals from an ISA are straightforward – though there may be a minimum amount you can withdraw and a minimum amount you must leave in your ISA account. If you take money out, you can only reinvest the difference between the permitted maximum and your original investment; so that if you originally invested £7,000 and later made a withdrawal, no reinvestment can be made in that tax year.

In principle, what you invest through an ISA should form part of your overall investment strategy: an ISA is no more than a method of packaging assets in a tax-efficient manner. But there are two implications to this approach. One is that ISA investments, especially if they are equities, should represent core long-term holdings. The second implication is to make maximum use of the tax-efficiency. It is possible, for example, to put zero preferences into an ISA: you would not pay any tax on redemption but there would be no income savings as zero preference shares and bonds do not pay dividends. For this reason, ISAs are especially suited to higher-yielding equities and to bonds, and many investors who put money into ISAs have done so through one of the unit trusts which specialise in these. So what does it cost to set up an ISA?

How to Save Costs

A £7,000 investment is a considerable outlay and in today's low inflation environment the annual percentage of total return (taking income and capital appreciation together) will probably be in single figures – unless you are very clever or very lucky. That in turn means that costs matter, above all in the early years of an investment: a typical estimate is that, if you put £7,000 into an equity or bond ISA, £400 or more will disappear in the first year as a result of the initial charge and the annual management fee. Some investors buy their ISAs direct from a fund management company in the belief that this is cost-effective; in reality, it is almost certainly not.

There are two ways to keep costs down: the funds super-market or the discount broker. In a fund supermarket, a large number, probably several hundred, funds are made available in a single ISA at a lower charge than the fund managers'. A manager will often make a 5% initial charge plus an annual 1-1.5%; a fund supermarket will make an initial charge of about half that. The discount broker works by handing back some or all of his initial commission and nowadays, thanks to growing competition, some of his annual loyalty rebate. These rebates are often given in the form of extra shares or units; where this would put the investor above the £7,000 annual limit, then there is a straight cash-back. It is even possible, by shopping around, for an investor to obtain a discount through a management group which makes no initial charge and also has a low annual fee.

ISA Performance

Buying shares or units through an ISA is no different from buying in any other way – except, crucially, that the investment may be relatively large. For many people, the answer here is to invest in an ISA by monthly payments throughout the fiscal year. This method – pound-averaging to the professionals – also solves the question of timing, especially given the barrage of ISA offers which appear in the media during the few weeks before April 5 every year.

CAT Standards

When the Labour government introduced ISAs and abolished PEPs and TESSAs, it also brought in CAT (Charges, Access and

Terms) standards. While this sort of scheme has worked well in stakeholder pensions, it is now largely an irrelevance in the world of ISAs. On cash ISAs, for instance, the minimum deposit or withdrawal should be no more than £10 and the interest rate offered should be no more than 2 percentage points below the Bank of England base rate. Financial providers have moved well beyond this sort of criteria: many providers now do not even try to comply and investors generally ignore CAT standards. But you should look carefully at the commission basis and read the small print.

Building an ISA

In putting together an ISA, you should use your basic invest-ment techniques. Risk probably comes first, with equities offering the greatest risk but potentially the greatest reward over the medium and longer term. Risk also affects bonds: bond funds enjoyed a wave of popularity when equity markets went into decline post-2000 but some investors seemed to be going after high yields – perhaps not always realising that a high yield generally points to a high risk.

Volatility is the next most important. An investment may perform well for a time, but go through periods of major ups and downs; you have to ask how much volatility you can accept in one year. If you are volatility-averse, you will have to raise the fixed interest content. This is especially important if the ISA is meant to pay off specific obligations, such as a mortgage or school and university bills.

Dividend Question

Income and capital gains generated by an ISA are free of tax (but there are limits on the time you can hold cash in a self-select ISA) – while the concession on dividends is under threat. At present, managers can claim back the 10% tax credit that comes with dividends, but the Chancellor has stated that this conces-sion will end after 5 April 2004 for ISAs and PEPs. Instead, consider convertible stocks or even starting to switch to bond funds; there are also some attractive distribution bond/equity funds, which can reclaim tax so long as they hold at least 60% in bonds.

Time to Change

Remember that you are not tied to your ISA. Many retired people will have a portfolio of PEPs, a TESSA-only ISA and several ISAs from different years. These may come to represent an important proportion of your total savings and it is important to keep them under review. Accept that an ISA is a wrapper, not an investment in its own right, and that no investment should be bought, and locked away and forgotten!

Poor performance, or the change of a successful manager, makes it risky to "buy and forget". An investment choice which seemed sensible only a short time ago may now look less appropriate. Above all, your own objectives may change; in particular, you may want to move from equities to a heavier weighting of fixed interest. As a later section shows, change has also become much easier.

Do-It-Yourself ISAs

The DIY, or self-select, ISA was created by competition among providers allied to the capabilities of the internet. Self-select ISAs are mostly offered by stockbrokers, as opposed to the fund management groups and they offer a wide choice of investments together with flexibility on the timing of sales and purchases. The investor's choice is as wide as in ISAs – UK and international shares, unit and investment trusts and bonds, which can be bought from different managers. The investor who chooses a self-select ISA has to determine his strategy: in the more difficult conditions that pertain to the equity market, self-select has often been used for pound-averaging, i.e. drip-feeding money into the market say a month at a time. There is one drawback to self-select ISAs, namely the Inland Revenue restrictions on investment in cash. If a self-select investor wants to stay out of the equity market for a while, two alternatives are fixed-interest funds i.e. gilt-edged or bond funds. Tax is charged at 20% on interest paid on cash balances. You can hold cash so long as the ultimate objective is investment. You may have to debate the time period with your inspector: six months was one criterion, but this may become more flexible if markets fall. Administration of a self-select ISA will probably be contracted to a stockbroker, who will charge around 0.5% a year. It is important, as ever, to identify any other fixed or transaction charges.

Don't Miss Your ISA

The appeal of a tax-free ISA is now widely accepted, and one of the features of the financial world is the rush of tens of millions of pounds looking for an ISA in the last few weeks of March and the early days of April. Many managers make efforts to accommodate the apparently large number of people who have not been able to make up their minds or maybe have just forgotten. Internet and the telephone are the most useful for tardy ISA investors; post can be subject to delay and strikes. Fund managers often accept debit cards while cheques do not have to be cleared by the end of the financial year. Despite all the market problems of recent years, these late rushes are probably a tribute to the popularity of the ISA; with its tax-free status, guaranteed by government at least to 2006, there does seem to be a view that virtually every tax-paying home should have one!

With-profit Bonds

Judged in terms of investor support, with-profit bonds stand out as easily the most appealing investment. In the last two years for which data is available, investors placed £27 billion into with-profit bonds to make a staggering total of £300 billion plus. By any standards, this is an impressive performance – but the providers of with-profit bonds are attacked for concealing charges, for penalising people who wish to cash in during early years or when markets are under pressure and for under-stating the risks of their investment policies.

The Sandler report of mid-2002 proposed a wide-ranging overhaul: insurance shareholders would no longer take 10% of investors' bonuses, the fund manager would be paid a fixed fee, the smoothing of investment returns would be spelt out, charges overall would be capped and – most important for higher taxpayers – the ability to defer tax on 5% annual withdrawals would be abolished.

Anyone thinking of buying a with-profit bond faces some important issues: if you do go ahead, make sure that you can withdraw without penalty if the rules are changed.

How They Work

A with-profit bond is, formally, a single premium investment bond which is offered by around 20 major insurance companies and friendly societies. When you buy a with-profit bond – we will examine later how you should buy – you invest in the insurance company's unitised with-profits fund. These funds are typically invested on similar lines to most pension funds and generalised unit and investment trusts – a large part in UK ordinary shares, some overseas shares, fixed interest securities, property and cash. Different companies vary in their investment strategy, especially in the relative holding of fixed interest as opposed to equities, so before you decide it is worth looking at the latest report and accounts or at an industry-wide survey.

The return on your investment comes through annual and terminal, or final, bonuses. Companies normally declare their annual bonuses at the start of the calendar year for twelve months ahead; the bonus is then added to your investment, gradually over the course of the year, hence the term "with profit".

Returns are 'smoothed' in this way, which means that some profits are held back in good years so that the companies can still pay out – though maybe at lower rates – when the stock market goes into decline. This smoothing process represents a significant part of the appeal of with-profit bonds: by contrast with the peaks and troughs of the stock market, the with-profit bond will show a progressive return – though remember that this return will grow faster in some years than in others. The terminal bonus is paid when you decide to cash in your bond. Its size will depend on market conditions and how long you have held the bond.

Appeal – and Some Doubts

The stock market declines of 2000 and later led many people to take the arguably safer alternative of with-profit bonds. Assume that you agree with this approach and stand ready to invest. Just before you commit, you need to address two of the principal complaints which are made against bonds – that their charges and their performance are less than transparent.

On charges, you will not see the details of initial and annual charges which are set out by unit and investment trusts, unless this is changed following the Sandler report. The insurance companies set out a reduction in yield which is caused by charges. You need to look at this carefully: to set an order of magnitude, you may find that an indicative yield of 6% is reduced to 5% after charges. That reduction represents a 16% cut in the return – assuming you buy direct from the company.

Performance Compared

What matters, you may say, is not so much transparency as how the with-profit bonds performed in fact. One of the independent groups within the industry carried out a five-year survey; this showed that with-profit bonds emerged close to equity unit trusts, lagging behind equity income trusts but ahead of corporate bond trusts. With-profit bonds showed much less volatility over recent years than these other sectors; and one guesses that a comparison over 2000 and later would favour with-profit bonds when the others would have been in neutral or negative performance.

That looks encouraging for with-profit bonds, but there is an important snag. Such performance figures would look very different for investors who wanted to cash in, above all during the early years of their investment; they could also look different for higher-rate taxpayers who faced a liability on encashment.

How to Buy

We need to look later at cashing in and tax in detail. At this stage, assume that you have decided to invest; you now need to choose your insurance company or friendly society and you need to consider how to carry out the purchase. You may have a favourite insurer; if not, you need first to look at financial strength. Some analysts look at companies' free asset ratios, which indicate the size of reserves from which companies will pay future bonuses. As an alternative, you can look at the credit ratings given to companies by one of the major agencies, such as Standard & Poor. It has already been suggested that you look at their portfolios to see if these fit in with your ideas; you should also look at their charges data – the reduction in illustrated yield – together with their performance over the years. You can also compare maturity or surrender values among different companies' bonds.

You have chosen your insurance company; what you should now do is go to a discount broker. This is exactly the same basis as using a discount broker to buy ISAs or unit trusts – except that the discounts at present are rather larger: initial discounts of 4-5% on an average investment can be expected – a discount of this size can have a significant impact on performance, as measured by the yield differential. Sandler's plans would mean important changes: a cap on charges would reduce the commission paid to advisers.

First Steps

The discount broker's refund to you will probably be added to your initial investment. On top of that, the insurance company will probably offer an extra allocation for larger investments: after all, it costs them no more to process a £30,000 investment than one of £10,000. So you start at day one with a bond worth, say, 102-105% of your initial investment. Each year from then on the value of your bond is increased by the annual bonus rate; over recent years, these rates were generally in the range of 4-6%, but the setback in worldwide equity markets is having an impact.

Early Cash-in

Everyone, notably the company and your broker, will have emphasised that with-profit bonds should be regarded as a medium- and longer-term investment. This means very much what it says. Insurance companies will make deductions from your investment if you cash in during the first five years. In your first year, the deduction could be as much as 9%, tapering to zero in year six. This is one of the offsets you have to consider against the smoothness and performance of your with-profit bond; if your circumstances change and you find that you need the money, then you face a penalty. Your only alternative would be to try to borrow on the policy.

Market Value Adjuster/Reducer

Even after five years, you may find that you cannot cash in your policy without a penalty: this is the Market Value Adjuster (called Market Value Reducer by some of the franker companies) which the insurance company can apply in order to deter too many bondholders withdrawing their cash. The Equitable Life story, when the company applied a significant Adjuster, brought this concept into the public arena. The insurance company defence is that the Adjuster is needed to protect the investor who wants to stay in as compared with the one who wants to cash in when the market is performing badly – which is just when many people want to realise.

After the two years of market decline in 2000 and 2001, many insurance companies were applying the Adjuster. Companies often waive application of the Adjuster when small annual withdrawals are made from the bond and on maturity and death. Even after five years, you should enquire about the company's Adjuster policy before taking an irrevocable decision to cash in.

Tax-free Annual Income

This is a crucially important area: for many years you have been able to withdraw 5% a year free of current tax. Sandler has suggested that this concession be stopped, which would make with-profit bonds much less attractive. If this is important to you, as it is to many people, then you need to pause until this position becomes clear. (When this was written, the Treasury were still pondering.)

For higher-rate taxpayers, a yearly withdrawal of 5% of the original investment, for up to 20 years, is treated as a return of capital and tax is deferred. As a return of capital, this payment does not affect any other benefits, such as age allowance under the income tax rules: this annual 5% is simply not income.

Remembering that there is no personal liability to capital gains tax on a with-profit bond investment, the tax attractions (if they continue!) are worth careful consideration. There are even more: the theory of the investment bond centres on the fact that it is tax paid at the standard rate of tax. That means for a standard rate taxpayer there will be no further liability on income withdrawals or on encashment.

Even if a higher-rate taxpayer goes above the 5% yearly withdrawal, he will not have to pay 40% on the extra; he only has to pay the difference between standard rate (already covered) and the higher rate, which amounts to 18%. The only caution for standard rate taxpayers is that their withdrawals might put them into the higher tax bracket or that the excess may affect their age allowance.

(As every perceptive investor will see, there is an investment assumption here: that your fund is growing by 5% or more a year; that we will examine shortly.)

Top Slicing

With-profit bonds are not attractive to non-taxpayers as the standard rate deductions cannot be reclaimed. (Non-taxpayers need investments which pay gross.) They are free of further tax to standard rate taxpayers, but higher rate taxpayers have to pay tax based on the Inland Revenue's "top slicing" system when they cash in their bond. Top slicing, like so many tax concepts, is in theory simple: if you are a higher rate taxpayer, you take your gain on cashing in, divide by the number of years you have held the bond, and that represents your taxable gain. In more detail, you take your cashing in figure, add any previous withdrawals; you deduct your initial outlay, any additional top-ups you may have made and any excess over the 5% a year allowance.

The good news, as we have seen, is that a higher rate taxpayer is not taxed at 40% but at the excess over standard rate, which is 40%–22%=18%. For standard rate taxpayers there is no further tax to pay, but you should consider whether this top-sliced gain may put you into the higher tax rate bracket; if that happens, you pay 18% on the amount you now have in that bracket. The Inland Revenue theory behind all this is that you pay tax in the year you cash in, but you are allowed to average, or slice, the gain over the years you have held the bond.

... And a Thought for Higher Rate Taxpayers

A tax rate of 18% may seem a relief to higher rate taxpayers, but it is possible not to have to pay even that. Many bonds are bought in joint names by husband and wife, and in many instances the husband is a higher rate taxpayer while the wife pays standard rate. In that case, the husband will pay the 18% higher rate on only half of the top-sliced gain.

It is possible to carry this logic one stage further, for the husband to give his share of the bond to his wife shortly before cashing in. Even if the gain puts her into the higher rate tax bracket, her average tax rate is likely to be less than the husband would have had to pay. In earlier years, the husband may be in the position of paying higher rate tax while he is working but moving on to standard rate when he retires. In that case, he will make no major withdrawals after taking out the bond; if he does withdraw, then he will keep withdrawals to the permitted 5%. Once he is retired, if he pays standard rate tax, he can cash in his bond without facing any further tax bill; the transfer to his wife will appeal to a higher rate taxpayer.

But Can They Now Withdraw 5% a Year?

With-profit bonds smooth out investment returns, but the underlying portfolios do not escape stock market setbacks. Reflecting the difficult market conditions of recent years, many companies have cut their bonus rates to below 5%. While 5% a year currently tax-free for 20 years is extremely attractive, if you withdraw more than the company's bonus rate you are eating into your capital. There is a further potential issue: some companies reserve the right to charge the Market Value Adjuster/ Reducer if you withdraw more than the bonus rate which they have declared. If you need the 5%, you may face an extra charge.

Are With-profit Bonds for You?

With-profit bonds will appeal to more cautious investors, who want part of their portfolio to be protected from the ups and downs of the stock market. Many investors will vividly recall the technology crash and the general stock market downs of 2000 and later. With-profit bonds will also appeal to higher rate taxpayers, especially those who expect to come down to basic rate on retirement. Higher rate taxpayers will also be attracted by the present ability to draw a current tax-efficient income of up to 5% a year. But here, it is important to underline the caution in the previous paragraph: bonus rates were reduced following the market setback, typically to below 5%. Apart from the Market Value Adjuster/Reducer, this means that income can be kept at that level only by eroding capital.

Perhaps most important of all, with-profit bonds are not a good investment for savings which you might need within the next several years: there are the built-in penalties for cashing in during the first five years and then the Market Value Adjuster/ Reducer which the company can apply if you want to cash in at a time of falling markets. Sandler's plans, if carried out, would greatly change the status of with-profit bonds; if you want to buy now, make sure that you can withdraw without penalty – in case Sandler's plans become law.

Using the Bond Principle

The bond principle is most widely applied to with-profit bonds, in which UK investors now have large holdings. But there are a number of other types of bond, of which you should be aware. Among these are distribution, guaranteed and offshore bonds.

In every case you make a lump-sum investment in a fund managed by an insurance company or friendly society. There is minimum life cover and the returns are free of tax to basic-rate taxpayers. Higher rate taxpayers can (at present) withdraw 5% of their capital free of current tax for up to 20 years; at the end of that time they pay tax at 18% (the difference between higher rate and basic rate) and their surplus is taxed on the "top-slicing" basis already described – in effect the overall gain divided by the number of years for which the bond has been held.

Distribution Bonds

The principal difference between these types of bond lies in their objectives. The popular with-profit bond aims to supply an effective total return on the basis of a smoothed progression. The distribution bond is used to generate income which is paid out half-yearly, or sometimes quarterly.

The asset make-up of a distribution bond differs from the with-profit bond with a much heavier bias towards gilts and bonds, generally to the extent of 55-60%. The balance of equities and property aims to provide further income and capital growth. (Unit values as well as income can go down as well as up.)

Capital + Income

The original aim of the distribution bond was to enable investors to draw income while keeping their capital intact. These bonds were especially attractive to higher rate taxpayers who moved on to basic rate tax when they retired. (As we have seen, an alternative for higher rate taxpayers is to gift the bond to their basic rate taxpaying spouse shortly before maturity.)

Other features of the distribution bond tend to follow those of the with-profit bond: the investment minimum may be rather lower at £5,000 rather than £10,000 in some cases. Charges on a distribution bond can be expected to reach 5% in total over the initial five years plus an annual management charge of 1%. There will also be withdrawal charges in the first five years, though, again, perhaps rather smaller than in with-profit bonds.

Yields Fall

Distribution bonds, from the mix of their portfolio, tend to be lower risk than with-profit bonds – though there is no guarantee that your initial capital will be maintained. The traditional answer was that you were bound to win: if interest rates fell, your capital value would rise while if rates rose your income would improve. Alas for theory, the later 1990s did not work out like that. Interest rates were dramatically reduced, above all in the USA, but capital values did not rise because markets were concerned about political risk and the prospect of company insolvency.

Pressure on Value

Typical yields on distribution bonds are generally in the range of 4% which compares favourably with banks and building societies – which was one of the main initial objectives. And for basic rate taxpayers who are prepared to tie up their capital for a few years and accept some capital risk, distribution bonds remain an investment worth considering.

For higher rate taxpayers, the recent years' fall in yields has reduced the appeal of distribution bonds. A higher rate taxpayer will want to draw his 5% a year of current tax-free (subject to Sandler!) income throughout the life of the bond – he can miss a year or two, as this concession can be carried forward. Once the yield on the bond falls below 5%, a withdrawal at that level means a reduction in capital – this is exactly similar to the higher-rate taxpayer who holds a with-profit bond and sees the bonus rate fall below 5%.

Tax – The Principal Appeal

For all these reasons, distribution bonds have become less popular among investors over recent years. But for a retired investor who is looking for an alternative to bank deposits over a several year period, the tax advantages of a distribution bond still have appeal. For a basic rate payer, returns are free of tax while for higher rate payers the tax rates are significantly reduced. There is a capital risk, so that anyone interested should look carefully at the track record. As ever in this market place, use a discount broker.

Guaranteed Bonds

For investors who wish to avoid capital risk, there is the option of buying guaranteed bonds – normally guaranteed capital growth or guaranteed income. As these bonds eliminate risk (depending on the status of the guarantor) some people use these bonds as collateral for borrowing.

These bonds have the merit of simplicity: when growth is guaranteed, a single premium secures a specific amount at the maturity date. This is in effect the long-established single premium endowment, with the important difference that growth is guaranteed and the product comes in the tax-efficient wrapper of the bond. With guaranteed income bonds, a single premium secures a guaranteed income – paid yearly or twice-yearly – until maturity, when the original premium is returned.

Higher Rate Tax to Basic

The main appeal of the guaranteed bonds will be to investors who pay higher rate tax while working but will pay basic rate tax on retirement – and who want the certainty which is comparable to a bank deposit. These bonds, like the others, are inflexible to the extent of carrying penalties on redemption in the early years – so that an investor can miss out on a rise in interest rates or a gain on the stock market.

Guaranteed bonds do best when bought at a time like the late 1990s when interest rates were about to go into steep decline. Anyone who bought these bonds and retired over those years will have made a sound investment.

One final word: do shop around if you are interested in this product, do use a discount broker and do take care when you compare the rates which are on offer. The headline rate may be shown before tax whereas payments will be made to you net of basic rate tax. Above all, do read with care the terms of the guarantee; this is a classic case of the advice that, if you cannot understand a financial product, don't buy it.

Offshore Bonds

Thanks to successive pieces of legislation, offshore bonds (Isle of Man, Channel Islands, Eire or the Caribbean) are no longer of general interest to UK taxpayers – some insurance companies in fact restrict their offshore with-profit funds to non-residents only. But these bonds can be useful to a number of people.

Offshore guaranteed income bonds, for example, pay gross interest which is rolled up into the capital of the bond. In this way, the bond could be helpful for people who plan to retire abroad. They may also appeal to non-residents living in the UK who pay tax only on income which is generated in this country – these offshore areas are outside the UK for tax purposes.

These bonds can also assist where the investor stands in the opposite position – having worked overseas but planning to retire in the UK. They will provide a sound investment, which should be cashed before you return to become a UK tax resident. There is an analogy with the offshore roll-up fund, which will attract people who can build it up during their working life and cash in after retirement when their tax moves from higher rate to basic – or they transfer to a spouse who pays basic rate tax.

Bonds and Bond Funds

Government and company bonds are the outstanding investment success story over the last few years. Over the 1990s as a whole, investment-grade bonds out-performed ordinary shares; by the end of the decade, bonds were still offering 5-10% yields while equities were going down.

What is a Bond?

A bond represents debt, a borrowing carried out by a government, an inter-government agency or a company. The bond will carry a fixed rate of interest and there will generally be a fixed date by which it must be repaid, usually at its face value, or par. Interest is generally paid twice a year and the bonds of interest to investors will be listed on a recognised stock exchange. A bond can be secured on the company's assets, or by a guarantee – or it may be unsecured. Government bonds carry simply the guarantee of the issuing government.

Bonds are issued throughout the world, by governments and companies of varying standards of financial strength and with different types of guarantee. To cope with this variety, an internationally accepted ranking system has developed: AAA stands for highest quality, such as UK or US government issues; in descending order follows AA, A and BBB. The latter, BBB, is regarded as the lowest ranking for investment-grade bonds. There then follows high-yield bonds, BB, B and C – which is the lowest, known by its American name, junk.

Bond Funds

Bonds, in particular the gilt-edged bonds issued by the British government, were the main savings outlet for Victorian pensioners. In recent years, many pensioners have invested in bond funds: these are unit trusts which hold a variety of bonds and have been offering yields in the range of 5-10%.

There is a simple truth about bonds: in general, the higher the yield, the greater the risk. So bond funds offering a little over the Bank of England base rate will probably hold investment-grade BBB bonds or better. A fund offering, say, double the Bank of England base rate may hold nothing but high-yield bonds, maybe some from emerging markets say in the Far East. In this case, you get exactly what you pay for, though some experts believe there is little point in holding a bond fund which offers little more than fixed deposits with a bank or building society.

Capital Choice

The reason for this experts' view is that a bond fund carries capital risk. While a bond carries a stated repayment date, a bond fund comes with no guarantee. The price of units in a bond unit trust depends on its yield, its success in picking good quality bonds, and so on. When buying a bond fund (or a bond itself if you may have to sell before maturity) remember that a rise in interest rates will bring a fall in capital values. A recession will also bring lower values, as the risk of default increases; we all recall Enron, whose debt featured in several London bond funds, and the default by Argentina where a national risk went wrong and hit many German and Italian investors.

Spreading Risk

The great appeal of the bond funds is that they spread risk by diversifying. If you buy a bond issued by a company, you have put all your eggs in one basket which contradicts one of the basic rules of sensible investment. Until your bonds are finally redeemed, the value of your investment depends on interest rates and the financial standing of the company. In the final analysis, you have the risk of default, in which case you may lose all your capital.

Research and analysis is the other advantage offered by pooled investment vehicles. Judging the status of a bond is not always straightforward. If the market rating is out of date, or about to change, you need to look at cash flow rather than profits (as you would if you were buying shares) and you need to examine whether, for example, the company has a major shareholder who will enhance its credit rating. Links of this kind were essential for assessing telecoms debt, but the information is not always easy to access for the private investor.

Lower Costs

The bond funds also offer lower costs and greater convenience for smaller investors. If you buy a bond, and wish to place it in a tax-free ISA – an attractive combination of high yield and tax-free status – then you will have to set up a self-select ISA, which tends to be rather more cumbersome and expensive. If you invest in a bond fund you will also have the option of a regular contribution rather than putting in a lump sum at a particular time. Pound-averaging, as this is known, can be a very successful investment procedure which cannot be carried out if you buy a single bond. Nor are bond fund charges especially high: one of the largest makes no initial charge and takes 1% a year, though some funds at this level levy penalties if you withdraw your investment before five years.

Fund Queries

For the great majority of investors, except for large players, bond unit funds as opposed to bonds will prove the most practical solution. But you have to remember, that, unlike bonds themselves, the capital is not guaranteed, and many fund values weakened in 2000-2. Nor is the yield guaranteed; the yield is what is generated by the underlying investments, so that an Enron will bring yields down. Rises in interest rates will reduce funds' values, which will not happen to a bond if it is held to maturity.

Performance

You need to look carefully at fund performance before investing, especially if you want to draw a regular income. Many of the statistics used in the industry assume that income is reinvested whereas the picture will look very different if income is withdrawn. Over one five-year period recently a group of corporate bond funds showed a 33% return if income was reinvested but only 5% if the income was taken out.

You also need to examine how yields are presented: normally two are quoted, the income or running yield and the redemption yield, which takes into account capital gains or losses if the investments were held to maturity. You may see a redemption yield quoted which is lower than the income yield; this means that there will be capital losses on repayment.

What Sort of Fixed Interest?

To go back to the Wall Street formula referred to right at the beginning of this chapter on page 57, someone aged 60 will want to have 60% of his portfolio in fixed interest securities, and that proportion will increase over the years. The key question is how this 60% should be divided between lower-yielding bank deposits, which are safe from capital risk and higher-yielding bond funds, where capital is not guaranteed.

There is, alas, no simple answer. Out of the 60% in fixed interest, it makes sense to keep a part which is available at short notice without a risk of capital loss. That suggests that perhaps 20% out of the 60% should be placed in instant access accounts.

For want of a better choice – and this choice must depend on the investor's feelings and judgment – the other 40% could be divided equally between bank accounts with notice periods (offering better yields than instant access) and corporate bond unit trusts. Following this logic, one should probably divide the 20% in bond funds equally between the lower-yielding lower risk and the higher-yielding funds which look beyond investment grade assets.

Bonds + ISAs

Bonds and ISAs make an attractive combination, and it was when PEPs – the predecessors of ISAs – were opened to bonds that the boom in the market began.

Corporate bonds and ISAs go so well together because of the compounding effect; suppose you put your £7,000 into a bond fund paying 8%. With tax-free compounding, your £7,000 would be worth almost exactly £12,000 after seven years. If, on the other hand, you want to withdraw the income of £560 a year tax-free, the bond funds offer quarterly or monthly income rather than the traditional half-yearly. This is beneficial to your cash flow.

Equities v Bonds

The final word has to be: do not get carried away by bond yields, which look especially attractive at a time when equity markets are volatile. Bank deposits which offer you capital protection do not offer any capital growth; in theory, bond funds should offer you capital growth if you buy at a time when interest rates are about to start falling – but as we have seen, this neat prospect can be confused by market fears of defaults. Going into fixed interest as a temporary resting-place while you make up your mind is one thing, but the Wall Street equity/fixed interest formula recognises that, from historical data going back two centuries, equities beat fixed interest over most five-year and (hitherto) over all 10-year periods.

Friendly Societies

Britain's 200 or so friendly societies are a distinctive feature of the financial scene. In the last century there were 27,000 registered friendly societies and even by the 1940s they counted around 14 million members. They provided cover in times of ill health and so lost much of their role with the creation of the welfare state. But governments cast a benign eye over friendly societies (most recently in the Act of 1992) which have retained a modest tax advantage – hence their possible appeal to retired people.

Tax Concession

Anyone can take out a 10-year policy with a friendly society where premiums are paid into a tax-free fund and the proceeds are paid out tax-free at the end of the term – unless you want to extend. The less good news is that the premiums are limited, to £25 a month or £270 a year. Some societies offer a practical alternative: a lump sum payment of around £2,300-£2,400 is placed in a taxable fund which then feeds money into the tax-exempt fund to make up the total £2,700 over 10 years.

The investment produces a tax-free cash lump sum along with a small amount of life cover.

How the Plans Work

Friendly societies are relaxed about age qualifications and will often allow investors to start a plan up to age 70 or 74. The plan is set for 10 years (friendly societies are officially directed into long-term investment) and you have the pleasure of becoming a member of the society. Joint policies may not be available but you and your partner can have a separate plan each. You then decide how much you want to invest up to the official maximum – though the society itself may set a minimum of say £15 a month just to keep down the costs of administration.

Your savings will then be invested in a general-purpose unit trust or will be allocated units in the society's with-profits fund. This works just like any other with-profits fund, with the society aiming to provide a smoothed rate of increase from a typical mix of shares, fixed interest, property and cash.

Keep for 10 Years

Many retired people would regard the life cover as redundant, but it has one advantage: if you die before the plan matures in

10 years, the society will pay out the higher of your life cover and the value of your savings. That apart, plans are geared to your saving for 10 years: if you stop saving, life cover stops though the value of the plan will continue to grow so long as growth is greater than the society's charges (of which more in a moment). You may be able to stop saving and then re-start, but that will depend on the society's decision in your particular case. Cashing in early is not an attractive option; in the early years in particular you may get back less than you paid in and you could be subject to tax if you cash in when less than three-quarters of the term has expired – i.e. 7½ years out of 10. On the positive side, your friendly society will almost certainly be a mutual, so that all distributed profits benefit policies linked to the with-profits fund.

Bonus Additions

Once again, these work in the traditional insurance way: bonuses are added by increases in the unit price. The society may well pay a terminal or final bonus to balance values among plan holders. By the same logic, however, the society may enforce a Market Value Reduction (or Market Value Adjustment, as made famous by Equitable Life) if it believes that actual return on investments is not enough to support the bonus additions. This prospect was very much in people's minds when markets started to fall in 2000, though it would be unusual for a society to enforce a Market Value Reduction at maturity or earlier death. However, try to be positive. Remember that the fund is progressing entirely free of tax on both income and capital gains.

Who Should Invest?

Friendly societies' tax-exempt status, modest though it is in value, means that their primary appeal will be to higher-rate taxpayers. The advantages, if any, of friendly societies' mutual status will depend on the investor's personal judgment. All the available profits go to policyholders rather than shareholders, but shareholders can arguably act as a spur towards greater efficiency. For retired people, the life insurance part of the package is of limited value, as we have seen, but grandparents always have the option of paying towards their grandchildren's plan rather than starting their own. As a plan holder, you will also have access to the society's other products, notably single premium bonds and critical illness and permanent health insurance.

Performance

Before investing, you should examine the society's performance record, on which general public data is somewhat limited. One recent analysis of 47 societies showed a small decline over one year (less than the fall in the market as a whole) and roughly no change over 3 years. Over the previous 5 years the average return was in the range 20-25% which falls into the category of sound rather than inspiring.

Against this, one of the leading societies compared the annual returns on £25 a month over a 10 year period: the building society return was 3.3% while the friendly society returned 9%, which is close to the average return on equities over recent years.

Charges Matter

Anyone thinking of a friendly society investment must pay careful attention to the level of charges. Because the government rules limit the amount of investment, the impact of charges may be significant – above all in a low inflation, low return environment.

Take as an example the charges spelled out by a leading friendly society. In a typical case, 96% of each savings amount is allocated to the with-profits fund. In addition to that implicit charge, there is an initial fee, a regular charge for the cost of life cover and a small monthly administration charge, which may be dynamised in line with retail prices. In this case, charges amounted to some £600 over the 10 years; given the relatively small amounts being invested, that would bring investment growth down from say 7% a year to just over 4%, which by any standards represents a significant reduction.

Tax-free Appealing, But . . .

The tax-free status of friendly society investment is appealing, especially to higher-rate taxpayers. The two issues are performance and charges. Performance has to be, as ever, largely a matter of judgment in the light of the society's record and its current spread of investments. Charges are easier to assess; they are set out and any investor should test them out against a possible annual return of say 7%, and maybe one higher and one lower figure. If the results are satisfactory, and you are prepared to put your funds aside for the 10 years, there is a case for going ahead; and the friendly societies offer official supervision and therefore a low degree of risk.

Financial Services Authority

The government has expanded and rationalised the forms of official assistance which are available to private investors. After legislation in the late 1980s, the government brought in the Financial Services and Markets Act, which now governs the investment scene.

How the FSA Works

The Financial Services Authority regulates all financial services firms in the UK. There have been criticisms that it can be too cautious and too slow, and there can be a problem over its ability to control foreign firms which sell shares to investors in this country – the Continental "boiler rooms". But the FSA has wide-ranging powers, which can be useful to an investor who faces problems.

The Financial Ombudsman Service is likely to be of more frequent and immediate help to investors: this is a single independent service for resolving disputes between consumers and financial firms. This service is free.

The Financial Services Compensation Scheme – which, it is to be hoped, you will not encounter – has the power to compensate investors in the event of failure by an authorised firm. This scheme covers claims against firms where they are unable, or likely to be unable, to pay claims made against them – generally when the firm is insolvent or has gone out of business.

How to Complain

Procedure is very important to all official bodies; if you do have a problem, you should know how to act. The first step is to telephone or write to the firm involved setting out your problem. If you telephone, confirm your conversation in a letter. Keep a copy, and of all further correspondence, and make a note of any telephone conversations; when you write, it is probably a good idea to use recorded delivery. Address your letter to the Compliance Officer at the firm.

You should reasonably soon receive a reply from the firm acknowledging your complaint and setting out the way they will deal with you. This should be along the lines of: a reply within four weeks of your complaint or a letter telling you what progress they have made. After a further four weeks they should give you a substantive response to your complaint; if that reply fails to satisfy you, you will be free to go to the Ombudsman service – and the firm's letter will give you their address and telephone number.

If you are still unhappy after eight weeks (the two 4-week periods), you will need to complete a form for the Ombudsman which they will supply or you can download from the internet. Send that to them, with supporting copies of all correspondence, notes of telephone calls, etc. – and use recorded delivery.

Do not hesitate because you regard the amount involved as small or because the firm's error is a minor one.

How the FSA Can Help

As well as handling complaints, the FSA has an important role – helping you to make the right investment decision. They operate a telephone helpline, supply free booklets, a consumer website and tables comparing the financial features of different products. There is, however, one very important thing which the FSA does not do: it does not recommend any particular company or product.

How to Choose

This leaves you with a major decision to make: which product and which supplier? The answers are familiar, but this is so important that they are worth setting out. Your first decision is strategic: do you want to make up your own mind or do you want to put the question in the hands of an adviser?

Choosing an adviser is discussed elsewhere in this book; you will probably go down that route if you feel out of your depth and/or the financial area does not interest you. Before you make this strategic decision, you will talk to friends. That is a sensible thing to do, but do remember that their financial situation may be very different from yours, so that their priorities and their targets are different. It is difficult to advise someone without knowing their full financial position; in the same way, it is often difficult to understand someone's decisions without knowing all the facts which led them there.

Making Up Your Mind

If you decide that you want to make your own decision – many people prefer to make their own mistakes, rather than suffer from someone else's – then a first step could be to collect data from the FSA. This will be wide-ranging and reliable and easy to understand – even if it stops short of specifics.

Once you have decided on the nature of the product you are going to buy – a with-profit bond, a tracker fund, whatever – you should shop around. You should collect information from several suppliers, whose details appear in advertisements or in the specialist financial pages of the daily and Sunday press.

You can read books like this: through books and the press you will gain access to views and information which may not be comprehensive and may not always be accurate – but they are disinterested. Those writers generally have no interest in whether you buy one company's bond or another – or do something completely different. Such unbiased advice can be extremely useful.

Always Ask

If you follow the adviser route, it makes sense to check that the firm is authorised to give you financial advice. Whatever the firm itself may say, you can telephone the FSA helpline and find out. The FSA rules require firms to be honest, competent and financially sound, and a part of the FSA's function is to take action when their rules are not being kept. The regulations protect you in different ways depending on what you are buying and also how you buy it.

Always remember what the FSA can and cannot do. It is the

financial watchdog to safeguard your interests; because of that role, the FSA is not selling anything. It cannot recommend a supplier or product; for that you need to go to an adviser or make up your own mind.

The FSA does not currently regulate mortgages, current or deposit accounts, credit cards, loans or general and medical insurance. In future, the Sandler report on retail savings wants the FSA to spend more on education – such as telling consumers what questions to ask before buying a financial product.

Chapter 3:

Pensions and Annuities

Your State Pension

Virtually everyone reading this book will receive a State pension. For many retired people it represents their principal source of income.

Pensions are paid to men when they reach the age of 65 and to women from the age of 60 – but the age for women is being raised. Women born before 6 April 1950 will continue to receive their pension at 60; those born after 6 April 1955 will get their pension at 65 – there is a sliding scale in between.

A wife who is not entitled to a State pension in her own right can apply for one based on her husband's contributions once he reaches 65, and this becomes her pension income.

Who Gets the Pension?

The basic pension is based on your National Insurance contributions. To get the full-rate basic pension you must have contributed for about 90% of your working life – currently a maximum 49 years for men and 44 years for women.

The State pension is paid weekly and many people arrange to have it paid into their bank. It is paid without any deduction of tax, so you have to include the State pension in your tax return – you don't have to include the winter fuel allowance and the Christmas bonus, which are free of tax.

When a pensioner reaches 75, he gets a free TV licence followed by a derisory pension increase of 25p a week at age 80 – though the government have now added an extra £100 winter fuel allowance for the two million or so pensioners aged 80 or over, equal to nearly £2 a week.

If your only pension comes from the State, you will not have any further tax to pay – unless you hold savings or property. If you get a company pension from your former employer, you will find that your tax coding is arranged so that they deduct the tax which relates to your State pension.

SERPS

The second tier of your State pension is SERPS, the grandly titled State Earnings-Related Pension Scheme. SERPS was introduced to provide earnings-related benefits for employed people. But if you were a member of a company pension scheme, you will probably have been contracted out.

The generosity of the SERPS scheme has been steadily reduced over the years, and it has now been replaced (though the sums you have built up will be safeguarded) by the State second pension (S2P), which focuses on the lower paid and people with long-term disability. At present, only employees are allowed into S2P.

Postponing Your Pension

When you receive details of your pension entitlement, you will be offered the chance to postpone your pension in return for a higher payment. At present, a man can postpone for up to five years and gets an extra 7.5% for each year he defers – from 2010 the terms will become more generous.

Is it worth postponing? After all, you are being offered an extra 7.5% a year which is comparable to a bond fund and comes from the State. Against that, it will take you time to catch up on the income you postpone, and for most people the appeal of cash in hand will be hard to resist. Postponement is suitable for people who have other income and no pressing outlet for their funds – or where taking the pension (especially if you are still working) would push you into a higher tax bracket.

Pension Credit

From October 2003 the minimum income guarantee is replaced by the pension credit. This has two aims. First, to provide a basic income for pensioners, and this is accomplished by establishing a minimum weekly income of £103 (a bit higher than under the previous system) for single pensioners and £160 for couples, and then providing an income top-up for anyone whose total income is below this. The other aim is to give limited extra rewards to people who have built up their own retirement savings, and this is done by paying a savings credit, which is set at 60% of savings income, but only up to a limit. The maximum income from both sources is £139 for a single pensioner and £204 for a couple.

The way in which these two benefits interact is extremely complex, but, for most readers of this book, irrelevant. Single pensioners with a total income above £139, or couples over £204, do not qualify for any benefits at all. Others should check the figures with care, and seek advice if in doubt. Do not add to the one third of pensioners who, it is estimated, do not claim their full entitlements under the present system!

Married Women's Entitlement

In order to obtain the maximum State pension, a married woman needs to have worked more than 38 years; if she has less than nine qualifying years, she will not be entitled to a State pension in her own right.

But once your husband is over 65 and has claimed his retirement pension, you will receive the dependant's addition. If you already receive a small State pension, it will be made up to the dependant's figure. But if your own pension is already larger than the dependant's, there will be no change.

Widows and Divorcees

One useful rule here is that a widow or divorcee under 60 can be credited with her former husband's National Insurance contributions. But take care: the rules also provide that if you re-marry before age 60, the credit is lost.

The financial argument is that you should postpone re-marriage until after age 60. Once you have started to draw a State pension in your own right, your position will not be affected by re-marriage.

Both this benefit and the married women's entitlement should be put into effect automatically.

Working After 65

For many people, reaching retirement age does not mean the
same as retirement. If you do decide to go on working, you have
the advantage that you do not have to pay any more National
Insurance contributions but your employer will still have to pay
National Insurance on your account.

Improving the State Pension

The State pension provides an income equal to just under 20%
of average earnings. The pension is increased in April each year,
normally in line with retail prices.

Some people regard that level of increase as less than generous, for average earnings rise faster than prices. To improve
pensioners' position, the government has announced that the
increase in the State pension will never be less than 2.5% a year.

The practicalities of collecting your pension have changed
recently: if your pension is paid into a bank account, it was
previously paid 4 or 13 weeks in arrears. It can now be paid
weekly in advance (the same as for people who take their money
in cash every week); but you must ask. Pensioners who take
weekly cash will be encouraged to open a bank account or a post
office account. You will no longer be able to get someone else to
collect your pension on an odd occasion. For pensioners taking
weekly cash, these changes will take up to two years to imple-
ment. (People who become pensioners will now have their pension paid into a bank account.)

Check the Figures

It is always a good idea to check the amount of pension which
you are being paid. It has been known for pensioners to be
under-paid.

Annuity Questions

An annuity is an income for life, which is paid to you by an
insurance company in return for a cash sum. The rules which
govern annuities in the UK are rigid. Pension savers are compelled

to buy an annuity by the age of 75 whatever their own circumstances or the state of the market. Once they have bought an annuity, pension savers will find that they cannot change: their annuity has no transfer value. Finally, they will discover there are severe restrictions on the amount of their pension savings that they can pass on to their heirs. What brought these anomalies into focus, and led to some innovative thinking in the annuity market, was the fall which took place in interest rates during the 1990s. Annuity rates are linked to the yields on government securities; the drop in these yields meant that annuities fell 40% between 1990 and 2000: a savings portfolio which would have brought a pension of £10,000 a year in 1990 would bring only £6,000 a year by 2000.

Deferring Annuity Purchase

There are clear risks in deferring a decision until the legal deadline of 75. You may well need the money; by the time you reach that age you may find that your portfolio has failed to perform and especially that the annuity market may have moved against you: imagine the feelings of someone who postponed an annuity purchase decision from 1990 to 2000.

There are two ways to defer annuity purchase, though it must be stated that both will tend to appeal to people who have larger savings, where the amount available is into six figures. First is an income drawdown contract and the second is a phased retirement pension plan.

Income Drawdown Contract

This first appeared in the mid-1990s. Essentially, it allows savers to keep part of their funds invested while drawing an income. To begin with, you have to decide how much you want of the tax-free cash which is available from your fund; normally, this ranges up to 25%. The rest of your fund is invested until you reach the age of 75 (or buy an annuity earlier), and from this fund you draw your income. The amount of income you can draw is fixed by the Government Actuary: the maximum is roughly what you would get in the open market for a standard annuity and the minimum is 35% of that. You choose where your fund is invested which means that your security is only as good as the fund's investments. You are free, at any time, to use your fund to buy an annuity but you cannot make further contributions to your drawdown plan once it has begun – you can make contributions to other plans.

Bequests Under Drawdown

One feature of the drawdown plan is that you can leave your pension capital to your estate. This is an unusual and appealing feature, but it comes at a price: if you are married, your spouse can cancel the drawdown after your death and take the pension fund as a lump sum – but, that lump sum is subject to tax at 35%. And the survivor must decide within two years whether to take this option. (The government has indicated it may tighten the rules from 2004.)

While drawdown brings flexibility, it does not avoid the cut-off at age 75. By the time you reach that age, you must have used up all your fund to buy annuities. And the rules also lay down that you must take at least the minimum income every year, on which you will pay tax as earned income.

Phased Retirement

Drawdown provides one major possibility for flexibility in the run up to age 75. The second – also somewhat complex, as pension plans tend to become once you start to move away from standard annuities – is a phased retirement pension plan.

Phased retirement plans can be set up from age 50 to age 75; they allow you to cash in your pension fund in stages, and you choose how much to cash in and when. Once you commit a part of your fund you can receive up to 25% in tax-free cash plus an annuity. In the early years the tax-free cash will provide a large part of your total income so that your overall tax liability will stay low. As time goes on, and you keep buying annuities, so their accumulated income will become larger.

There are two essential differences between drawdown and phased retirement plans. In drawdown, you must take your tax-free cash – or as much as you want – at the start. In phased retirement, your tax-free cash is paid over a period and forms part of your income. The second difference between drawdown and phased retirement is that you can still make contributions, if eligible, to a phased retirement scheme but that is not allowed under drawdown: you have to start another scheme.

The Path to 75

You may choose drawdown or phased retirement as you approach your 75th birthday but you may feel that they are too complex – which means that they will be more expensive – or your fund is not the right size. You need to modify your investment position as 75 approaches – otherwise you are betting that the value of your investments and the state of the annuity market will be optimal on your birthday. One way to do this is to go more liquid within your fund, generally in the years before 75. Some insurance companies will do this for you as a matter of course, but if you are holding shares or unitised investments, you will need to take action yourself. The other approach is to take out an annuity, or even a series of annuities, say in the years between 70 and 75. (If you start earlier, annuity rates will be less attractive and you may not require the income.) This approach is like pound-cost averaging in buying investments and represents a reasonable way of spreading risk. If you want to back your own judgment, then you have to decide the future trend of interest rates; if you believe that interest rates, and therefore annuity rates, will be rising as you approach your 75th, then you should hold back on your earlier annuity purchases. Conversely, if you think that rates are falling, then you should buy your annuities sooner rather than later. That being said, interest rate forecasting is outstandingly difficult. The more cautious, or the less self-confident, will split their fund into three and buy annuities at age 70, 72½ and finally at 75.

How to Buy an Annuity

You have decided to buy an annuity using your pension funds; perhaps you are near 75, or perhaps like many people you are taking the decision some years earlier as you have finally decided to retire. To buy an annuity requires an initial simple decision: are your situation and your requirements fairly straightforward, or complex? If your position is simple, you can take the decision yourself, or with minimal and therefore low-cost advice. Basic annuity rates are published in the press and in specialist money magazines. If you have access to the internet, you will find a range of information. You are, basically, looking for the best price offered among the major insurance companies. If, on the other hand, your pension fund has an unusual history or what you want is out of the ordinary then you need specialist advice. If in doubt, do not economise: this is one of the most important financial decisions you will make. In some cases, you will pay no more by using an adviser as opposed to going direct to the insurer – who may build the commission into the values he quotes.

Decision Time

You have identified your provider and you have a quotation, which will probably be good for 14 days. You now have to make a series of decisions regarding the nature of the annuity which you are about to buy. The first decision is whether you want a pension that will benefit the surviving spouse or partner. This does not have to be your wife or husband and it may even be possible to name any spouse in case of re-marriage. In the majority of cases the pension is bought by the husband with a pension payable to the wife in the event (actuarially likely, assuming similar ages) that he dies first. There can be some latitude in the amount of pension to be paid to the survivor: it can be the same income, or a proportion, say 50% or two-thirds. This is an important decision – clearly personal – because a partner's pension, if bought by the husband, is likely to make a significant reduction in the initial level of his pension.

To Escalate – or Not Escalate?

Your starting point is a level annuity, where the money income you receive is fixed for the rest of your life. This will give you the largest income to start with, but the snag is inflation: even if price rises are kept to the official target of 2.5% a year, your pension will have lost around a quarter of its buying power by the end of 10 years. So you may decide that you should have escalation, so that your pension rises by a pre-determined amount each year. But there is a trade-off: the greater the escalation, the lower your initial income. It is possible to arrange escalation which keeps up with retail prices. Alternatively, you can arrange what is known as limited price escalation which means that your pension keeps up with inflation up to 5% a year; or you can arrange a fixed rate of increase, say 2%, 3% or 5%. There is something to be said for taking a level annuity, which gives the highest starting income and build up a savings portfolio probably through an ISA for the medium and longer term, say in equities or index-linked investments. That does require a certain amount of financial self-discipline!

Case for a Guarantee

Related to the question of whether or not to escalate is the issue of a guarantee, or 'years certain' for which the pension will be paid. Under the traditional type of annuity this guarantee – allied to a spouse's pension – is one of the few ways to benefit your estate. Many people opt for a five-year guarantee, but ten-year ones will be available in return for some reduction in your initial income. You do not have to take a guarantee but most people will choose to do so. In the absence of a spouse's pension and/or a guarantee, the pensioner's early death will mean a big 'win' for the insurance company.

There are a few other, less important, decisions you will have to make. You will have to decide how often you want to receive your pension – monthly is probably the most popular choice, but you can opt for quarterly or annually. This needs to be considered along with another timing question: whether you want to be paid in advance or in arrears. As always, there is a trade-off in terms of your initial income but this only becomes significant if you choose an annual pension: the difference in income between annual payment in advance and arrears could well be in the range 7-10%. If you do choose an annual pension, you also need to consider proportion: an annuity with proportion will be paid pro rata from the last payment to the date of death. If you have an annual pension and die shortly before the payment date, your beneficiaries stand to lose a significant amount if you did not take an annuity with proportion.

Special Rates – "Impaired Annuities"

Special rates annuities are a little-known section of the market, in which a number of insurance companies specialise. Essentially, these are special rates for smokers or for people with a record of ill-health; the theory is that, because your life term may be reduced, you can expect an improved annuity. If you come into this category, you should seek advice. The good news is that you may get a useful increase in your annuity over the norm. The bad news is that the administration becomes more complicated involving you, your adviser, your doctor and the insurance company.

Moving Away From Standard Annuities

Standard annuities remain the most popular choice in the market-place. They are familiar, and they are safe; you know your income position.

Against this, they offer limited flexibility and little benefit to your heirs – none at all unless you choose a guaranteed payments period and/or a spouse's pension. And the fall in annuity rates since the early 1990s has reduced their appeal – especially to people with larger pension funds who were prepared to tolerate rather more investment risk. These people opt for investment-linked annuities, which come in three sorts (in ascending order of risk): with-profit annuities, unit linked annuities and self-invested annuities.

Three Investment Options

With-profit annuities are most simply understood as taking an annuity from an investment bond. The investment mix will be similar, that is around 60% in UK and overseas equities and 40% in fixed interest, real estate and cash. In this form of annuity, you have to select a rate of bonus: if you choose nil, then your income will never fall below your starting level. You may, though, decide to anticipate some bonuses, which will improve your initial income; but if the actual bonuses declared by the insurance company fall below what you anticipated, then your income will fall.

You probably need advice – as with all three investment options – because conditions vary among insurance companies. You may, for instance, want the freedom to switch to a standard annuity if interest rates rise: with higher interest rates, annuity rates will improve, while higher rates may adversely impact on a share and bond portfolio.

Unit-linked Annuities

Unit-linked annuities are next stage up in terms of risk – and, to be fair, in growth potential. And they may be marginally more expensive to operate.

In this case, you choose a growth rate within a range offered to you: the lower the rate you choose, the lower your initial income, but the greater the possibilities for the future. Above all, there is no floor: if the units perform less well than the growth rate you have chosen, then your income will fall.

You do not own units – they are simply a method of expressing the income from your annuity. And like every annuity, a unit-linked plan cannot be transferred or cashed in. For many people, it probably makes best sense to operate a unit-linked annuity alongside a standard annuity or an occupational pension; to rely wholly on a unit-linked annuity is a high-risk decision.

Self-invested Annuity

Top of the pile for risk has to be the self-invested annuity. This is riskier than the unit-linked annuity just as buying individual shares is riskier than investing in unit trusts. On the optimistic side, the benefits of successful stock selection can be considerable. A self-invested annuity is for larger funds, content to face investment risk and probably alongside a standard annuity to provide some certainty.

Benefits for Your Heirs

Annuities are a fast-moving scene and have probably seen more change in the last ten years than in the previous twenty. The developments from standard annuities just outlined came out during the 1990s. But all of the plans above suffer from a grave defect for pensioners: you can pass on none, or little, of your pension assets to your heirs. Even more recently still, an intriguing solution has been found – but, please note, it is relatively costly to operate and is open only to funds above £250,000 and when handled by independent financial advisers. It is called the Open Annuity.

The Open Annuity – How it Works

The key feature of the open annuity is that the unused part of your pension funds can go to your estate on death. This represents a major step forward, though the procedures are necessarily complex:

Step 1:   You set up a self-invested annuity, with investments chosen by you or by your fund manager.

Step 2:   You buy a share in the insurance company which is making the provision using other assets; as a result of this investment your estate can obtain the surplus in your pension fund when you die. As with any self-invested annuity, you select your level of income within the set limits, and the range of investments is the Inland Revenue approved list.

Complexities arise because an open annuity represents, in effect, an individual annuity which is not permitted in the UK by Inland Revenue rules. (Why, one wonders?) But individual or segregated annuities are permitted outside the UK, and the Inland Revenue simply requires that the insurer must be within the European Union. Ingenious minds solved the conundrum: the insurance company, which is UK-owned, is for example based in Gibraltar, which permits segregated annuities and is within the EU.

The open annuity is the first annuity which allows annuitants' funds – or the remaining surplus – to be inherited. That represents a great step forward: but the charges are relatively high, the minimum size is significant, the scheme is IFA-access only and it operates on a self-investment basis. For pensioners with larger funds and some appetite for risk who have reached 75 and are compelled to take their decision, the open annuity offers considerable advantages.

Ordinary Annuities

All of this discussion so far has been in terms of pension annuities, or compulsory purchase annuities. As was explained at the start, these are the annuities which you have to buy with your accumulated pension fund some time before your 75th birthday. There is an alternative, namely the ordinary or purchase life annuity. This is where you decide to use your own money, quite apart from the compulsory purchase, to buy an annuity. The important feature of ordinary annuities is that they carry significant tax advantages.

The tax break arises because the Inland Revenue considers a part of each ordinary annuity payment to represent a return of capital – known as the capital content – and this part of the payment is tax-free. The size of the tax-free capital payment depends on age and sex: it is higher for men than for women, and it rises with age. Moreover, the income element is regarded as savings, so that tax is deducted only at 20%. The overall effect is that a higher rate taxpayer in his mid-70s will pay somewhere around a 10% tax rate on his gross annuity payment.

This will appeal to pensioners who have no close dependants or whose dependants are provided for. It can be expensive to protect capital in a purchased life annuity – either agreeing a number of 'years certain' or ensuring a payback of all the amount invested.

Do You Buy When You Retire?

One particularly difficult decision is whether to buy an ordinary annuity when you retire. You are quoted a pension, along with a smaller one if you take the permitted 25% cash. As we have seen, the great majority take the 25% cash and use the money to celebrate, move to a new house or invest. But you could put the money into an ordinary annuity.

You would then be in the same position as if you had ignored the cash option and taken your full pension – except that you would be getting much better tax treatment on the cash element which had gone to acquire the ordinary annuity. (Some people invest the 25% if they retire early, and then use the money to buy an ordinary annuity in later years, when they will hope to get better terms.)

This looks irresistible – but there is a catch. Your pension from your employer will probably be inflation-proofed, at least up to 5% a year; it may even be fully index-linked. You could find it expensive to replicate these terms in the commercial annuity market; very expensive for full index-linking. There is no easy answer, except to say that tax-driven decisions are not often the best – and to begin, you need a forecast of inflation over the years to come!

If the amounts are significant, you need expert advice – and you could probably start with your former employer's actuary or personnel department.

Pickering on Pensions

Many people reading this book will be receiving a pension from their former employer. This will probably be a final salary scheme (also known as defined benefit), or it will be based on a money purchase plan (defined contribution) to which you and your employer will have paid and where the value of the plan buys your pension.

In mid-2002, when a number of employers had started to close their final salary schemes, the Government commissioned a report from Alan Pickering, former chairman of the National Association of Pension Funds. His two suggestions for final salary schemes would make them much less attractive to pensioners:

(a) Schemes need not include a widow's pension.
(b) Pensions need not be escalated in line – or at least partly in line – with inflation.

Government reactions are still being worked out: Pickering's proposals would only help to solve the 'pensions crisis' by making final salary schemes less valuable for people who retire in the years ahead. That in turn would make planning for retirement, and above all investment strategy, even more important.

As with the Sandler plans, so with Pickering: we shall have to wait and see.

Stakeholder Pensions – A Gift from the Chancellor

Anyone who has retired and has the resources available – indeed anyone over the age of 50 – should take a close look at a stakeholder pension. Someone who retires at the age of 60 and takes out a basic stakeholder pension until age 75 will have received tax benefits of more than £10,000. Benefits of this size from the Chancellor are all too rare.

New Style of Pension

The stakeholder pension, set up by the grandly titled Welfare Reform and Pensions Act of 1999, was intended to help moderately-paid people to make cost-effective provisions for pensions – with the unstated implication that the State pension might be inadequate.

So the stakeholder pension breaks completely new ground: under the traditional pension rules, which still apply, you need an earned income to provide a pension: 'relevant earnings' is the official term. But the stakeholder is open to the unemployed as well as the employed and the self-employed.

The stakeholder goes a step further – it can be financed by anyone to anyone. If you wanted a stakeholder pension, but couldn't afford it, a friend or relative could do it for you. You can finance a stakeholder pension for your spouse, your children and grandchildren and even for your next door neighbour. The stakeholder is extremely flexible and brings a tax advantage – whatever your tax position and even if you do not pay tax at all.

How it Works

Everyone who is eligible can make a stakeholder contribution of up to £3,600 a year. The tax benefit is given, at standard rate of 22%, direct to the insurance company which provides your pension. This means that you pay £2,808, and the Inland Revenue pays the other £792 to your insurer. In simple English, you get £100 worth of pension for a cost of £78; that represents the financial appeal of the stakeholder pension.

Nor can this benefit be swallowed up in charges: these are capped by the legislation at just 1% per year, and some pension providers charge even less. Flexibility extends to the operation of the stakeholder: you can stop and start again as it suits you; you can transfer your stakeholder to another provider; the minimum you can invest is set very low, as little as £20 per month.

Who is Eligible?

You have to be a UK resident; as we have seen, your tax status is irrelevant. There are three groups of people who are excluded:

1) Those who earn more than £30,000 a year and have a company pension plan – an occupational pension scheme; the stakeholder is aimed at the lower-paid.
2) Controlling directors.
3) Those aged 75 or more; the stakeholder is a pension fund and under the current rules you have to turn this into an annuity before your 75th birthday. People approaching age 75 might therefore think that there is little to attract them. That is not correct – immediate vesting (see below) offers an attractive option.

Stakeholder for Children

A stakeholder pension is so flexible that you can set one up for your children or grandchildren – you can even set up a stakeholder for someone else's children or grandchildren. (A child under 18 can benefit from a stakeholder, but cannot make contributions.)

When stakeholders were first introduced, some dazzling calculations were made to show how the tax benefits can accumulate – but there is a major problem. No-one can draw a pension from their stakeholder before the age of 50 (unless they are ill or follow a particularly demanding or hazardous profession). Most children will have more immediate needs, and there is always the risk that the rules may be changed over time – perhaps raising the minimum age from 50 to 55 or 60. (Already the government seems to be planning an increase to 55.)

The tax attractions remain, and children can make their own contributions after age 18 until they join an occupational scheme and earn more than £30,000 a year.

Investing the Stakeholder

Some people may stay away from a stakeholder pension in the belief that, if they take out a pension, they are committing to bonds or equities. This is an unnecessary concern: stakeholders are provided by the major insurance companies and financial groups which offer a wide range of choice. You will generally have access to an index tracker and a deposit fund as well as specialist US or European funds. You can choose what you think most appropriate and you will be able to change later if you wish to do so or if your circumstances alter.

Role of the Stakeholder

In addition to its tax advantages, a stakeholder is a useful way to bolster existing pension income. Take a married couple where the husband receives an occupational pension but the wife has only the State pension; it would make sense for the husband to take out a stakeholder for his wife, whose marginal tax rate is low. Take a situation where a person aged 60 has used his pension fund to buy a level annuity, where the money income is fixed, in order to maximise current cash flow. It could make sense for him to take out a stakeholder in order to add pension growth in later years.

This person could also gain tax-free cash: when you cash in a stakeholder, it works just like any other money-purchase pension fund which is used to buy an annuity: you can take up to 25% of the fund tax-free in cash. You have to use your stakeholder to buy an annuity by age 75, but under the flexible rules you can stop paying in at any time.

For the Over 70s – Immediate Vesting

If you are in your 70s, you will have only a few years until age 75 in which to enjoy the tax benefits of a stakeholder. You may therefore be inclined to pass by – which could be a mistake. You can use a stakeholder to buy an immediate income, on terms which are better than those offered by the banks and better even than the corporate bond funds. This is known as 'immediate vesting' and is open to anyone who can take out a stakeholder – even if they have no income outside their State pension and the money comes from a friend or relative.

Immediate vesting is an interesting concept: you hand the insurance company the maximum £2,808 which gives you a policy of £3,600. Your first step is to take your 25% tax-free cash which amounts to £900. At this point you have a policy of £2,700 which has cost you £1,908.

You then use this £2,700 to buy an immediate annuity, which will be level (i.e. fixed in money terms) and probably payable for five years certain. In other words, you have acquired a lifetime fixed interest investment – but on better terms than you can get elsewhere. To give an indication – and remember that annuity rates alter all the time – a man aged 70 could expect to receive an annuity of £240 or so a year before tax. On his outlay of £1,908 that represents a return of 12½% at low risk – the provider being one of the major insurance companies.

An Annual Exercise

You can repeat this exercise every tax year at steadily better rates of return as annuity rates rise – right up to your 75th birthday. Women can do the same, though their annuity rates are slightly lower as they live longer than men. Starting, say, at age 70 (the annuity rates are less attractive if you begin much earlier) you can build up a growing income stream at attractive rates of return.

One word of caution: you have to be aware of the impact of rising income on your tax position (e.g. via age allowance) and on any benefits you may receive.

Too Tax-efficient to be True?

This may all seem attractive, so you start to wonder: what is the catch? There is no catch, though you are dealing with a pension fund which will have to be converted into an annuity. This means that your decision is fixed for all time: in immediate vesting, for example, you earn an attractive return if you live long enough, but you have given up control of your capital. And for some people, the annual limit of £3,600 gross for a stakeholder will be modest in relation to their overall financial affairs. If you take out a stakeholder pension for someone else, you are making a gift of the money involved.

You may also wonder why the stakeholder and its possibilities are not more widely known about and discussed. The answer is all too simple: the government-imposed limit of 1% on charges leaves little margin for advertising, which is how providers market unit trusts and with-profit bonds. And for the insurance companies, there is an administrative burden in dealing with small pension amounts under the maximum of £3,600 a year.

The very attractions of the stakeholder scheme contain their own warning: governments do not favour situations where people can enjoy benefits from the tax system and are apt to legislate them away. The stakeholder scheme is only a few years old and carries a social-political objective – to provide a savings outlet for the lower paid. So far, the take-up has been modest; if the stakeholder plans appeal to you, you should probably act sooner rather than later – who knows how long the stakeholder's life in its present form will be?

Paying for Healthcare

About one in three of us, according to the current estimates, will need some form of healthcare. This book is not about health, but illness and its treatment have financial implications. For those who do want to make provision for healthcare costs, there are some insurance products.

Needing healthcare does not necessarily mean needing long-term healthcare, which is the most expensive. You can arrange for care to be given at home, you can move to sheltered housing or later to a residential home. State allowances, notably attendance allowance, are available which will reduce the cost – but almost certainly will not meet the full cost. It helps that your State pension will now be paid for your first year's stay in hospital.

Care Costs

It probably makes most sense, as in many financial exercises, to look at the worst case, if only to move back from that. Full-time care in a nursing home or residential home is reckoned to cost around £25,000 a year on average in the UK – though figures will be higher in London and the south east, and higher quality residential homes will also cost more.

If your doctor considers you need long-term care, the first point of reference will be your local authority who have an obligation to assess your needs. They will also carry out a means test: essentially, if you own more than around £20,000 of cash and investments you will have to pay until your assets run down. (Your house will not be included, assuming you live there with your spouse.) Local authorities vary a good deal in how they pay for care costs and provide care; if you are likely to be in this situation, it makes sense to enquire before the need arises. Since 2001, nursing care – but not personal care – has been free. There are also differences between England, Scotland and Wales.

Paying the Costs

Many pensioners will prefer to make their own arrangements for care. For some people, a one-in-three chance of needing care and a lower probability of needing long-term care may seem acceptable odds, and they will take no action. For people who expect to go to their local authority, there is one word of warning: do not try to get within the asset limits by giving away cash, investments, or even your house. Apart from the effects on your own financial position, this may well not work as local authorities have considerable powers to investigate. If the local authority decides that you were seeking to avoid care costs, you will be assessed as if the gifts had not taken place – rather like the Inland Revenue powers under inheritance tax.

Assume, then, that you want to provide for your own healthcare – or at the very least work out how you will pay if the need arises for your spouse or yourself.

Investment Route

Many people look at funding long-term care on a hypothetical basis, that they will meet the costs if they arise by using an equity release scheme to mobilise cash from their house. This is a reasonable solution, especially as the older you are, the better terms you will get. But it also represents a family decision and is therefore one you should discuss with your heirs.

An alternative, if you have the resources available, is to set aside an investment portfolio which is designed to meet your care bills. This should be low-risk with prospects for growth: one possible route is for you and your spouse to build a series of ISAs, either fixed interest or with a high fixed interest content. Another, if you are involved in buy-to-let, is to decide to sell property if the funding need arises. These calculations complicate tax, and particularly CGT and inheritance tax, planning; unless you stand to benefit from a trust, you may need to keep more assets under your control than would otherwise be the case.

Insurance Alternatives

Insurance plans will appeal depending on your attitude to risk and uncertainty – allied to your own and your family health history and any prognosis from your doctor. The basic form of insurance plan offers a fixed amount of cover in return for periodic premiums or a single premium. This represents the lowest-cost insurance option and carries out the basic insurance function of limiting your risk: the fixed cover payment will continue so long as you need long-term care. (Note that the payments will not apply to temporary care.) There is one major drawback: if you do not need long-term care, the premiums are lost. If you do not need to claim, there is no return of premium.

The next stage up in sophistication is a long-term care investment plan. Such plans combine long-term care insurance with an investment bond. If you do not claim, the investment value (or if you make small claims, the net figure) will be paid into your estate. Remember that this is an investment product so its value may fluctuate – and if it falls, you will have to add to your premium or see your benefits reduced.

These plans fall into two categories: the first, and more costly, protects your initial investment while the insurance company pays the benefit. In the second category the insurance company uses the investment to begin with in order to pay out claims and takes over the payments itself only when the investment element is exhausted. In this case, an agreed level of care costs will be met but there may be no investment value left at the close.

Long-term care insurance pays out when you can no longer carry out an agreed number of specified 'activities of daily living' (ADLs).

Immediate Care Annuities

Immediate care annuities are basically the same as traditional annuities: you pay out a lump sum and in return receive a pre-determined income – in this case for as long as you need care. As with traditional annuities, you can arrange a fixed money income or you can arrange to have the income indexed to the cost of living which will reduce the payments to start with. You can even arrange to have the annuity linked to an index above the level of inflation, for it is well known that healthcare costs rise faster than the average of retail prices.

There is a useful benefit under immediate care annuities, that the income can be channelled to the care provider so that you have no income tax liability. As you do not receive the income, your tax position is not involved.

The less good news is that immediate care annuities resemble ordinary annuities in another respect: there is no return of investment on death. It may be possible to arrange a guarantee period, or years certain, but this may be shorter for immediate care annuities than the 5 or 10 years which are possible under normal annuities.

Comfort is All

More than in any other single financial sector, being comfortable is most important in health insurance. Apart from the obvious medical issues, there are questions such as the need to make a will and to give an enduring power of attorney and the impact of your decisions on your estate. For some people, it is extremely important to be able to cap or limit the amount of healthcare costs. Others will look at the probabilities, ignore insurance and take some perfunctory steps in their investment portfolio. Long-term healthcare is pre-eminently an area where you decide what you want and therefore what you pay for.

Chapter 4:

New Investment Ideas

Ethical Investment

For many years, the Church of England was the major ethical investor: its large portfolio avoided shares in producers of alcoholic drinks, arms manufacturers, tobacco, commercial television and newspapers. For other investors, ethical or SRI (socially-responsible investing) was regarded as something of an indulgence to an individual taste.

In the 1980s, this began to change. Issues such as global warming and environmental damage featured in political debates; as people began more and more to take charge of their investments, they wanted to invest in accordance with their principles. A new type of investment was created.

Growth of Ethical Funds

Ethical investment is a natural for pooled vehicles such as unit trusts and their later development, OEICs (open-ended investment companies). Some undesirable investments were obvious, such as drink and tobacco, but otherwise the ethical nature of a company called for information and research which are more difficult for the individual investor.

The first ethical fund was launched in 1984; by the end of the 1980s there were about 10 and around 20 by the end of the 1990s. Now, there are around 50 ethical/ecology funds holding assets of about £5 billion. A turning-point came in 2000, when all company pension schemes had to declare their ethical policy as part of a statement of investment principles.

Performance Keeps Up

Now, ethical investments are available for lump sum transactions, ISAs and pensions including stakeholder pensions. A retired investor who wants to make an ethical investment has a wide range of choice.

The great concern over ethical investment was that it would lag behind conventional portfolios, as a number of attractive investments were excluded. While ethical track records are not all that long, these funds have in general kept up with traditional unit trusts; there is a sizeable spread in their performance but some funds have done well. A government minister, speaking at a 1998 conference, confirmed that, "Research currently under way in this field appears to suggest that ethical funds have performed better than other alternative investment approaches."

Ethical Choice

Choosing among ethical funds is particularly difficult: you need to take care to match their criteria and objectives with your own, and the funds' tests change over time. The first step in looking at ethical funds is to assess the three major categories, which are animal rights, humanism and the environment. Animal rights remain important, though as one ethical fund manager pointed out, a decade ago ethical funds were concerned almost exclusively with avoiding the fur trade and bloodsports. Humanist issues include oppressive regimes abroad, human rights, water and landmines. Environmental issues will feature pollution, preservation of forests and woodlands.

How the Funds Decide

While these are the principal areas for the ethical trusts' attention, the managers will then use one of two basic approaches towards investing. The emphasis will be between ethical funds and green or environmental funds. Ethical funds follow a range of criteria, while their main emphasis is on negative selection in order to avoid companies which are involved in certain areas – rather like the Church of England's original policy. After the negative screening, a positive vetting procedure is then applied. Green or environmental funds tend to follow a positive procedure, investing in companies whose products help to improve ecology or to clean the environment.

Light Green v Dark Green

There is then a clear difference between funds as to how strongly they apply their criteria. A 'light green' fund which takes a more relaxed view might, for example, rule out animal testing for cosmetics. A 'dark green' fund, which takes a firmer line, would avoid animal testing for whatever reason.

These tests might seem straightforward, but investment decisions are far from easy. For instance, cars and oil will appear on most funds' negative screens, but it is the major oil companies which are busy researching alternatives to fossil fuels and the car companies which are trying to make hydrogen-driven cars and trucks a practical reality. To decide not to invest in these companies will in principle hinder those efforts.

Thematic Investment

Thematic investment represents a much more difficult, but potentially interesting, area of investing in companies which represent the industries of the future. This covers a wide range – fuel cells, waste management, solar and wind power and water treatment. The possibilities are exciting, but the risks are high and often these will be small companies rather than parts of established groups. Small company investment can be rewarding, but in the short term at least their shares tend to be more volatile. The rewards for success can be great to set alongside the casualties – which makes this approach especially well suited to a unit trust.

Invest in the Best

This is a rather more sophisticated approach: a sector is considered, which the fund would normally avoid, but investments are made in those companies which are judged to be most progressive in improving their activities. The underlying theory is that investment will send a signal to the company's competitors and encourage them to follow the best company's drive in fuel cell research, etc.

This approach widens the range of investments open to the ethical fund and recognises that progress in many areas must depend on the work of the major companies – which might be excluded on an initial green list.

Engagement

For completion, one should mention shareholder action by ethical funds: nowadays, this tends not to be the disruption of meetings at mining companies and banks, which formerly attracted attention but probably irritated more investors than it convinced. With the growth of their assets, the ethical funds are now able to make significant voting representations at annual meetings and in some recent cases have been able to speak for 10-15% of shareholders.

Picking a Fund

Investors who wish to make an ethical choice and who also aim for their investment to grow in value probably have a choice of three main areas: locally generated electricity (the distributed power sector), water technology and waste collection and disposal. There are listed companies in all three sectors, though many of them rank among smaller companies; there are some larger plcs in waste collection, possibly because of the economies of scale.

Choosing the ethical fund which most closely matches your principles is not easy; there is some coverage in the financial press, and rather more on the internet. Otherwise, you have to write to the management companies and compare the annual reports. If you are prepared to pay in order to make a choice, you should go to an independent financial adviser, and there are some who specialise in ethical investment; the trade organisation will be able to guide you. Whatever your specific choice, you can now be reasonably confident that an ethical choice should perform as well as more traditional investments.

Protected Investments

Stock market setbacks in 2000 and later seriously concerned many investors. Most people remain convinced that equities are the optimum investment for the long term. The evidence is overwhelming: the latest is an American study that equities out-performed all other investments over 10-year periods going back to the beginning of the nineteenth century.

But successive declines in equity values have led to demand

for a new type of financial product – one which offered participation in equity price growth, but protected your original investment. Structuring such products was not easy: one of the objectives was to ensure that gains were subject to capital gains tax, where investors have an annual allowance and taper relief, rather than to income tax. Financial institutions have produced at least two types of scheme, one which offers (in practical terms) capital protection and the other which reduces the risk of capital loss. In each case, needless to say, there is a trade-off.

Aiming for Complete Protection

You invest in an insurance company offshoot for 5 years. This offshoot selects 30 leading blue-chip shares and you benefit from their growth over the five-year term. But the growth is capped at 100%. To explain: suppose that the portfolio consisted of three shares; over the 5 years, one of these grew by 130%, the second fell by 50% and the third grew by 40%. Growth on the first, and most successful, is capped at 100%, so that the average growth of the three emerges at 30%. If you had invested £1,000, you would get back £1,300. Capital protection is provided by the insurance company placing short-term funds with leading finance institutions; this represents the only, and probably theoretical, risk to you getting your capital back intact – that the insurance company itself gets into financial difficulties, or the same problems affect one or other of the institutions with which the money is placed.

ISAs but no Dividends

The insurance company arranges to have its offshoot listed, which means that you can subscribe through an ISA. That also means that you can switch existing ISAs and PEPs in order to invest, though you need to make sure that there will not be any significant switching charges from your existing provider.

An ISA will mean that you are free from capital gains tax at the end of the five years, but there are no dividends from this investment. Absence of dividends is typical of such schemes, but that represents an important part of the cost: if you bought the shares yourself you could expect at least 3% a year.

Cautious Investment

The insurance company will also commit itself to a cautious investment policy – such as ruling out short sales of shares. Charges will be moderate, probably close to the 5% initial and 1% annual which are typical of many unit trusts.

Flexibility is always important in this type of scheme – whether you will be able to realise your investment if your circumstances change before the end of the five years. This sort of scheme does not charge the deductions or market value adjustments which feature in with-profit bonds – but there are no guarantees. A secondary market will be set up where you can sell, or buy, the securities. But this market is unlikely to be active; the market maker may not deal at all times while the price and spread cannot be judged in advance.

A Bank Alternative

One of the leading banks has carried this insurance plan a stage further, also offering capital protection but in this case with 100% of the growth in the FT100 Index. Again, security depends on the other financial companies, banks or insurers which are involved in the scheme. Note that your capital is protected, as in the insurance plan, if you are prepared to hold the investment to maturity – up to six years in this case.

Once again, there is no income but the company is listed in Ireland so you can subscribe through an ISA, which would provide a tax-free capital gain if the stock market goes ahead. The bank has added an extra feature, so that the company is wound up if the index has risen 20% after two years or 40% after four years. You should decide to hold the plan to maturity, which will be the full six years, or two or four years if a rise in the index triggers a winding-up. If the scheme runs to its final six-year maturity, the payout will be based on the average of the index over the last 12 months.

Tying Up Your Capital – and Timing

Plans of this kind are appealing: investors who thought that equities were going nowhere for a number of years would not be interested – but that is probably a minority pessimistic view.

There are three drawbacks. First, there is no income. Secondly, you should be prepared to stay the entire course – five years in one case and up to six years in the other. If your circumstances change, and you need the funds, then in both cases you might have to realise at a loss, or try to borrow.

Lastly, any scheme of this type faces an inevitable averaging problem. It is fair for the bank or insurance company to take a 12-month stock market average before maturity, but in volatile times this could produce anomalies. Probably the most irritating would be if equities rose sharply during the last month of the 12-month averaging period; in that case, your average would be below the market level when the plan matured. You can also imagine a scenario where the stock market booms for several years, but then falls during those crucial last 12 months – and so on.

The answer to this problem would be to take out a series of plans, rather than make one investment which depended on a particular timetable. That complication represents part of the cost of a scheme which is trying to give you the best of both worlds.

Your Money Back – If

These two plans probably represent the nearest you will get to protecting your base capital – only governments can provide absolute security, and then not in all parts of the world.

If you are prepared to give up complete protection of your initial capital, and take a greater level of risk, there is another type of scheme which offers a high level of income or growth together with the return of your capital – on condition that a share index, or a range of indices, perform. These schemes tend to be shorter-term than the five or six year insurance and bank plans.

Yield or Growth

This second sort of plan will offer you a choice of high income or growth over a shorter, say, three year, period. Whether you choose income or growth – perhaps 10% gross a year income or 33% growth over the three years – will depend on your own requirements and your tax position. The plan may be structured so that the income comes in the form of dividends. If you choose income, this can be annual or monthly.

As in the previous plan, this is eligible for ISAs which means that the high income can be free of tax. If you choose the growth route, the possibilities are even greater as you can use the ISA along with your annual tax-free limit for capital gains tax. The way this works is that you invest the full amount of the ISA, namely £7,000, and sufficient outside the ISA, between £20,000 and £25,000, to generate a gain that falls inside your annual tax-free limit. In that way you invest a total of £30,000 and make a tax-free gain of £10,000. By the same logic you can transfer existing ISAs and PEPs into the scheme. For a couple the amounts double: but remember that joint applications cannot be made for ISAs.

Cashing in Early

A three year period is easier to deal with than five in terms of a possible change in your circumstances. The securities you buy will be listed (otherwise they would not qualify for an ISA) and there will be an appointed market maker. But if you have to sell before the end of the three years, there are no guarantees of cash value and the price you get will depend on the market and if there are buyers.

If you die before the end of the three years, the usual rules apply: the investment is transferred to your personal representatives or as they direct after probate. ISAs and PEPs automatically lose their tax-free status on the death of the holder, so the investment would be subject to income tax or CGT from the date of your demise onwards, as well as to inheritance tax.

What About Your Capital?

This is much more complex. Your capital return is tied to the performance of a share index (or maybe a group of indices), so that you may get back less than you invested. In this case, you get back all of your capital if the index never falls by more than 20% from its start point during the whole of the three years. You will still get your money back if the index falls by more than 20% but recovers to stand above its start point throughout the last month of the plan period. You start to lose capital if the index drops by more than 20% at any time and during the last month fails to match its original level. If the market goes into free-fall, and during that important last month the index lost more than 50% from its start point (a staggering fall in one month, but UK share prices fell by more than that in 1972-74) then you could lose all your capital.

Is it For You?

Assessing a plan of this kind is difficult, as your return depends on the relevant stock market holding steady over the next several years. Historical evidence indicates that equity markets will perform positively over a 10-year period, but the record is more erratic over shorter time-spans. And a plan of this kind is inevitably subject to an unexpected political disaster. These 'precipice' bonds suffered badly in the 50% drop in share prices 1999-2002, and many investors lost capital.

In the last analysis, you have to assess risk: a three-year or five-year plan offering attractive income or growth conditional on a share index is not suitable as the only or major component of a portfolio. If you have a positive view of equities, this sort of plan – especially when linked to an ISA – may have a place as the riskier element of a portfolio which also has a solid low-risk base.

Trading an Insurance Policy

Most of us will have taken out an endowment policy during our working lives, to pay off a mortgage or as part of a general savings plan with a particular commitment in view – school or university fees, or to provide a welcome 18th birthday present for the next generation. Many people continue their policies until maturity but some, for various reasons, surrender theirs back to the insurance company – and are probably disappointed by the low surrender value. In recent years, people have begun to accept that an endowment policy is essentially a specialised form of investment, where it was possible to offer policyholders who wished to realise a good deal more than the insurance company would give on surrender. A market developed for trading endowment policies, which is now a £10 million a week business, and is worth attention.

Selling an Endowment

Some retired people will have an endowment policy which they wish to sell: an endowment policy is one where the policyholder receives a bonus statement each year. Some endowment policies cannot be traded – those which are unit linked or tied to a fund management group. And the policy must have run for at least eight years and have some time still to go. If the policy meets these tests, you are looking at a possible TEP – a traded endowment policy.

You then go to a financial adviser or an intermediary who will seek bids from the market makers. After a week or so the intermediary will be back with the best offer, which could be up to 30-40% above the insurance company's surrender value. You are under no obligation to accept and you will be charged no fee: the intermediary will get his commission, probably around 3%, from the market maker. This explains the supply of TEPs, based on the estimate that policyholders in the UK have been losing between £150 million and £200 million a year by surrendering rather than selling.

Buying One

If this is a £500 million a year business and policyholders are selling rather than surrendering, then someone must be buying; some retired people will be interested as buyers in this new marketplace. To a buyer, a TEP stands for a low-risk investment offering a potentially attractive yield. When you think of buying a TEP you have first to consider how much capital you will spend; what level of premiums you wish to pay until maturity; how long ahead that should be, and if you have any preferences as regards insurance companies. The theory is simple: you buy the policy, take over the premiums and collect on maturity.

The details are that you enter into an absolute deed of arrangement and your interest is registered with the insurance company. You should plan on keeping the TEP going until maturity.

Cashing In

Once you have bought a TEP from the original owner (or possibly from a second or even a third owner) he gives up the right to all proceeds which arise on maturity. So on maturity of the policy, you receive all the policy proceeds including the sum assured, all of the declared bonuses and usually a terminal bonus. The surplus of that amount over the capital you paid and the premiums you continued represents your gain annualised over the period of years.

How Good is Performance?

Comprehensive performance data for TEPs is difficult to assess: one analysis of 15 policies which matured in summer 2002, having been taken out up to five years previously, showed annual compound returns ranging from 3.5% to 8%. All of these had been set up with leading life offices. (Out of the total 15, six showed in the range 3.5%-5% and nine between 5% and 8%.)

Compared with stock market performance over the same period 1997-2002, these returns stand out favourably, especially for what represent low-risk (if not very liquid) investments, where outlays ranged between £6,000 and £20,000. But the stock market slide of those years is still evident – only two out of the 15 policies achieved maturity values which matched the original estimates.

Taxation

From a tax standpoint, policies are divided into two types: qualifying and non-qualifying. The taxation rules are complex – the main test of a qualifying policy is that premiums are payable at least once a year with a life of 10 years or more, apart from term assurance. For an endowment policy, the sum assured must represent at least 75% of the total premiums for its term. All other policies are non-qualifying.

Qualifying policies are subject to capital gains tax in the year when they mature; you can set your individual allowance against the gain, or twice that if the policy is jointly owned with your spouse. Another option is to spread your investments to mature in smaller amounts over several years, so that you receive a series of tax-free gains in succession. Non-qualifying policies come under income tax, but there is no liability to basic rate tax. For higher-rate taxpayers, the gain is top-sliced, i.e. averaged over the period of years as for with-profit bonds. Here again, it makes sense for higher rate taxpayers to hold policies jointly with their spouse or to transfer them to a spouse, who pays only basic rate tax, shortly before maturity. Less good news is that the government threatens to tighten the rules on second-hand life policies.

Is a TEP Worth It?

A TEP is a low-risk investment offering a potentially attractive yield. But it may not be readily liquid nor tradeable. It is a situation where you should have resolved to hold the policy until maturity. Borrowing against the policy is possible if you find that you need the funds. Resale is another option.

One current uncertainty lies in the future of insurance company bonuses. Insurance companies suffered in the stock market decline of 2000-2 and were compelled to reduce bonus rates.

All this affects TEPs because purchases are based partly on estimated maturity values, and some of these could start to look optimistic. But your purchase price may be lower than the insurance company guarantee, which will at least avoid the prospect of capital loss.

TEPs are not necessarily high-priced – a purchase can cost from £5,000. And they are easy to operate: your premiums will be paid by direct debit and some insurers are prepared to accept a lump sum now in place of future premiums.

TEPs are a relatively new market, but worth looking at for someone who wants to build a diversified portfolio, is not deterred by novel ideas and is prepared to tie up capital for a number of years.

Shareholder Perks

About 70 companies offer perks to shareholders – cut-price goods and services. These are tax-free and some of them are quite large – including houses and cars. No sensible investor should buy a company's shares solely because of the perks which are offered – it is probably most practical to regard the perks as a kind of dividend bonus. But if you are attracted to the shares anyway, then the perks make a useful extra addition.

Cross-Channel Travel

Probably the best-known perks are those offering benefits to people crossing the Channel, either by ferry or Eurotunnel. But the range goes much wider, and anyone interested should contact one of the broking firms which maintains a list of what is on offer, along with the terms and conditions.

One housebuilder offers a 1% discount on a new house, in addition to any other promotions available; the UK's leading airline offers 10% off published fares for flights, plus 10% off holidays for the shareholder and up to three other people; a leading UK hotel group gives 15% off the total bill and 15% also off meals and drinks when non-resident, and so on.

Perks come in several forms, often a card or vouchers which give a price reduction. (Vouchers are often sent out with the annual report, so you need to watch the timing.) The minimum number of shares needed varies a great deal: some companies have effectively no minimum, specifying just one share. Other companies require a specific holding, which can run even into thousands of pounds. You also need to check whether there is any minimum period for which you must hold the shares, i.e. be on the register – the administration of perks is often handled by the company secretary or the registrars.

Nominee Question

You need to establish whether you will still receive your perks if you hold your shares through a nominee, which many brokers prefer. Most companies will allow the perks to carry through (they may need a letter from you) but not all – once you have placed your shares with a nominee, then the nominee becomes the legal owner while you are the beneficial owner.

Perks also change, and some household names have abandoned their perks plans – partly, one suspects, on grounds of cost, but principally because of the administration involved. Travel, along with hotels and restaurants, remains the most popular perk and several of the principal companies in these areas require a holding of only one share. But do get an up-to-date list and check out the points mentioned in the previous paragraph before you go out and buy the shares.

Chapter 5:

Financial Planning

Equity Release – Raising Money from Your Home

For many people who have retired, their largest single asset will be their home. The children have moved on, the mortgage has been paid off and property values have risen. But earning an adequate income in retirement has become more difficult than ever: the Chancellor puts an extra tax burden on pension funds, stock markets are volatile, annuity rates are falling at the same time that people are living longer. Many people find themselves under financial pressure while tens of thousands of pounds remains locked up in their own homes. Over the last 20 years, the value of the average house has increased four-fold.

What are the Options?

The first choice is to sell your home and move into somewhere smaller, possibly in the country or by the sea. Perhaps you can 'trade down', to raise cash but without diminishing your stand-ard of living! There is the financial attraction that any profit you make on selling your home – your principal residence – will be free of capital gains tax. But you may prefer to keep the home in which you have spent most of your married life; moving house will also mean costs and upheaval.

The next alternative is to take out a mortgage, probably in the same way you did when you first bought your house. You will then have a capital lump sum, to spend or buy an annuity; but you will also have monthly payments of interest and you need to consider how the loan will be repaid. The house could be sold when you and your spouse have died or moved into long-term care, or maybe one of your children will be able to pay off the mortgage and take over the house.

Equity Release

To meet these questions the financial sector has developed "equity release" schemes to enable pensioners to make use of the wealth tied up in their homes. The basis of many of these schemes is that they give you part of the value of your house in exchange for payment of interest or a share when you die (or go into long-term care). You can benefit from some of the locked-up equity in your home without having to move house or sell.

There are three sorts of equity release scheme, which are explained in this chapter. But the first point to note is that equity release is most appealing to people in their mid to late 70s and their 80s. Equity release schemes are open to people from age 60 or 65 but the values are not likely to appeal to you. The insurance or finance company which provides the funds will let you live rent free and will not get its money until you and your spouse have died – and that is reflected in the terms they offer.

Which Properties are Eligible?

The short answer is the great majority of traditional houses having a minimum value of £30,000-£40,000 and above – though to gain a meaningful benefit you should own a property valued at £200,000 or more.

Leasehold houses and flats are not likely to be accepted unless the lease has at least 75 years to run. Houses and flats built to an unusual or idiosyncratic design will not be popular – or valued at relatively low figures – while some lenders avoid Scotland. Conversion flats are likely to be less popular, for the same reason as they are difficult to mortgage. Any mortgage will have been paid off or reduced to a low figure, which can be resolved when the equity release scheme goes into effect.

Making a Choice

Before addressing the three main types of scheme, you have to make two decisions. One is what you want from the equity release scheme. Do you want to turn your house into a pension, or do you want a cash lump sum, or a combination of the two?

Your next decision is one to discuss with your family and in particular your heirs. Your spouse will be immediately concerned, but you must also appreciate that equity release will reduce the value of the home which you will leave to your heirs and it may well be that the house will have to be sold after your death – unless your family have sufficient funds to pay off the debt. Your family need to be aware of the choice you are making and its impact on your estate.

Roll-up Mortgage

This is one of the most popular types of equity-release scheme. It is a traditional-type mortgage, with the crucial difference that the fixed rate of interest is 'rolled up' and added to the loan so that you do not have to pay out of income. The capital and rolled-up interest are paid off when the property is sold. You have the right to repay early, but often early redemption carries a penalty.

A fixed interest rate means less risk, but some schemes charge variable rates. In this case, it is important to establish a minimum and maximum, otherwise, if interest rates rise, the debt could have grown to a large figure by the time the property is eventually sold. Check if there is a condition (which occurred in older schemes) that interest must be paid immediately if the debt reaches a certain proportion of the property's value. On the positive side, you may get a guarantee of no negative equity – the lender will not look to your estate even if the total debt rises above the house value.

The amount you can raise depends on your age and health: the older you are the greater the advance – and larger advances are also available to people in poor health. For a 70-year-old couple in average health, the scheme should produce 25-30% of the valuation of the share of the property you are pledging. If a couple with a £200,000 house took a roll-up mortgage for 50% of the property's value they could expect a lump sum of £25,000-£30,000.

The great appeal of the roll-up mortgage is that you do not pay out interest. All interest is rolled up and deducted from the final sale of the property after your death. The price for this is that interest is compounding all the time: if you took a lump sum of £50,000 and were charged 7% interest, that would have doubled over 10 years to just under £100,000.

Home Reversion

Like the roll-up mortgage, this type of scheme provides a lump sum. In a home reversion you sell all or part of your property. When you die, the part you have sold goes to the reversion company: if you had pledged 30% of the property, the reversion company will take 30% of the proceeds when it is sold. You do not have to make any repayments, and, by contrast with a roll-up mortgage, you are not charged interest: the reversion company makes its money by selling its part of your property after your death – and from the growth in value of the 30% interest in your home which you have sold to them.

But the reversion company will not pay you the market value of your property – as it has to wait for your death to make its money, the older you are the better terms you are likely to get. A 70-year-old couple in average health should expect around 40% on their share of a £200,000 property, so if they sold a 25% stake they would receive a lump sum of around £20,000.

Under home reversion, your heirs are sure of some assets – 75% in the above example. Under a roll-up mortgage, by contrast, they have to pay for interest compounding. If you sell a small share in your home to begin with, you may be able to go back later for a further sale. A home reversion is age-sensitive and you have sold part of your property. Under a roll-up mortgage, by contrast, you remain the owner.

Home Income Plans

Home income plans provide an annuity for your home. You take out an interest-only mortgage and the proceeds are used to buy an annuity. Part of the income is used to pay the loan interest; this is a purchased life annuity, so that the after-tax position compares favourably with a compulsory purchase annuity. The mortgage is repaid through the sale of the house once the couple have died or gone into long-term care. You may be able to generate a small amount of cash, especially to pay off an outstanding mortgage but the company's aim is to provide an annuity. This annuity may be fixed – a level annuity – and therefore subject to inflation; alternatively, some home income providers offer an annuity which is linked to the value of other properties in their portfolio.

It is possible to sell only part of your property as the basis for an annuity, so you retain a part of the equity. Annuities, once agreed to, may not be changed, so you need to have formed firm intentions. In any annuity, you – or your estate – will have made a bad bargain if you die within a few years of taking out the annuity; to meet this, a home income company may provide a capital sum if death occurs within the early years, in some cases based on a sliding scale.

Home income plans offer a regular income for the life of your spouse and yourself and they can ensure there could be some benefit for your estate. Against this, home income plans suffer from the drawbacks of annuities. Rates change and have fallen substantially over the past 10 years. To compare with the other schemes, a 70-year-old couple in average health with a £200,000 property could (at the time of writing) take a home income plan based on 50% of their property value, to provide an annuity income of £2,500-£2,700 a year.

Not So Good Old Days

Home income plans still suffer from the problems of the 1980s and early 1990s when house prices fell and interest rates soared. Some pensioners even had their homes repossessed because they could not meet the interest payments which were being demanded!

The major companies in the sector reorganised to form a self-regulating body – SHIP (Safe Home Income Plans) – to protect people taking out home income or equity release schemes. Members display the SHIP logo, and the scheme guarantees that you will never lose your home, that you will be free to move to a suitable alternative property if you wish and you will be given a clear and understandable presentation of your commitments.

Equity Release: The Practical Issues

You have discussed among your family the issue of using your house to improve your financial position. You have decided whether you want an annuity or a lump sum. You also need to concentrate on four important tests for any scheme:

1. You and your partner have the right to live in the property for life – which will mean until death or you are both in long-term care.
2. You are free to move house – this will be subject to conditions, so that if you moved to a smaller and less valuable house, some loan repayment may be made.
3. You receive your cash lump sum free of obligations, or an annuity from a major provider.
4. You receive a guarantee of no negative equity – there will be no burden to fall on you or your estate.

You should get a firm 'yes' to all four – if not, pause and re-consider.

And you will have considered what effect the lump sum or the annuity will have on tax and on any benefit you may be receiving – or may receive in the future, say under long-term care.

Step by Step

You are going to need a financial adviser – unless you have a close friend or member of the family who is knowledgeable and has gone through the procedure. You will certainly need a solicitor and a surveyor – though some of these costs may be repaid if you go ahead. You should allow 12 weeks from application to completion, and you should draw up a schedule of the costs you will have to meet.

If you start with a financial adviser, you should involve another member of the family – it is desirable for another member to attend all meetings with you, partly so that the family realise the implications and partly to provide help and a witness at the meetings – when there will be detailed exploration of your finances and your personal circumstances. You need a formal valuation of your home.

A solicitor is important, and you should employ one who has some experience in equity release. (If you are uncertain, approach the Law Society who will give you the names of local firms.) Your solicitor needs to take you through the contract you are signing. Under the rules for SHIP companies, your solicitor has to sign a certificate stating that the equity release company has explained the scheme and you understand the scheme and its conditions.

Your Obligations

You will have costs – if you employ a financial adviser (some equity release companies will deal only with intermediaries) you should discuss with him whether there is a commission and the basis on which he will charge you. Some schemes will refund at least part of the legal and surveyors' fees in their package; but remember that if you decide not to proceed, these bills will be to your account.

Once you have completed, your basic obligation is to insure your property and to keep it in good condition and preserve its value. You now have a mortgagor or a co-owner, whom you should contact if, for instance, you plan some major work, say building a conservatory. You also need to contact the equity release company if your personal circumstances change, say if your spouse has to go into long-term care.

Also bear in mind a possible future change in your situation: suppose your spouse goes into long-term care and a young relative moves in with you. The plan will end when you die or go into long-term care, when the house will probably have to be sold, perhaps leaving your young relative without a home. Or if you are single and marry after taking out a plan, you need to talk with the equity release company – otherwise, the plan may end on your death and your spouse may not be able to stay in the house.

IHT Benefit

Equity release schemes are tax-efficient as they reduce your bill for inheritance tax. You are either creating a mortgage debt on your property or selling off part of it, so your net estate will be reduced. How much you save depends on what you do with the money: if you give it to your grandchildren, for example, you have to live for seven years to escape IHT.

Is Equity Release For You?

Many pensioners need money to improve their quality of life, while at the same time owning a valuable house. Some pensioners have few dependants, or have provided for them, and could use the extra cash which equity release can provide.

Equity release is in fact being put forward as a solution to the pensions shortfall which is expected on a national scale over the coming years. Hundreds of thousands of employees, including many professional people, are expected to face a poor quality of life in retirement because they are not investing enough in pension funds. As house prices have out-performed shares over recent years, banks and estate agents are working on new property-based retirement schemes all the time.

Buy-to-Let

Buying flats and houses in order to live off the rental income was well known in the age of the Forsytes; buying-to-let then lost its popularity in the age of the equity and rent control. But in the past few years, buying-to-let has dramatically recovered its popularity: in just four years around the end of the 1990s, the number of buy-to-let loans exploded from just over 25,000 to just under 200,000, while the value of buy-to-let loans grew from £2 billion to almost £15 billion as banks, building societies and insurance companies rushed to offer finance.

Is Housing a Good Investment?

It is not hard to understand this boom. House prices continued to rise, even accelerating, at a time when stock markets were going sideways or down. Interest rates were falling, helping to underpin the rise in house prices and bringing lower yields on bonds and bank deposits – which are the traditional alternatives. Attractive loans were available from financial institutions, which were themselves looking for investment alternatives, while for many people self-management of properties offered an appealing and profitable occupation.

The starting-point has to be an assessment of house price prospects, especially for those who recall the falling prices and negative equity problems of the late 1980s and early 1990s. The principal reason for optimism must be that interest rates are low, so that interest payments now represent a smaller proportion of households' after-tax income than around 1990. Probably the single most important test is the ratio of house prices to average earnings. When that ratio gets too high, house prices will be vulnerable; when the ratio is low, house prices generally strengthen. Here, one has to say that the evidence is uncertain, which tends to suggest that a period of consolidation may be the most likely prospect.

The pessimists' counter is that house prices have become vulnerable to rises in interest rates. As inflation has fallen, people who hold mortgages, or debt of any kind, will not be able to rely on rising prices to reduce the real value of their obligations. And, with an aging population, demand for housing may fall and the level of buying and selling may also be reduced.

Regions Differ

That is the overall picture, but one that is to a degree unreal – unless you decide to invest in a property fund. Anyone attracted by buy-to-let has to choose a specific flat or house in a specific area with an investment of at least £100,000 of which he will have to put up a minimum £25,000. Not surprisingly, the explosion of buy-to-let offers at the end of the 1990s and the early 2000s led to some reduction in rents and above all to an over-supply position in some popular areas – parts of London, Glasgow, Edinburgh and some towns on the south coast.

You need to consider the market you are trying to exploit – young professionals or a flat or house near a university or a hospital. Do not forget the old adage of the commercial property world: there are three tests for a property, namely location, location and location.

You need to consider whether or not to use a letting agent, whose role is to know the area. There are tax advantages – see below – while many people are put off, often wrongly, by the apparently high level of charges. Above all, do not make the traditional mistake of "amateur landlords" – do not necessarily buy a property which is the sort you yourself would like to live in.

Affording the Risk

At first sight, the economics look attractive. Suppose you bought a house for around £120,000 (which is close to the average UK property price). At the time of writing, you could get a mortgage for less than 6% p.a. for up to 75% of the house's value; so you borrow £90,000 and decide, in logic, to pay yourself 6% also on the 25% which you put up. You are now paying up to £7,200 a year, and you have taken an interest-only mortgage on the basis that the rise in the capital value of the house will take care of the repayment in 20-25 years' time.

You assume an 8% return on your investment, so you have a margin of 2% overall. This looks reasonable but you need to focus on practicalities and possible financial pitfalls.

Managing the Practicalities

You have chosen your property. You have to find tenants, check their references, collect the rent, maintain and insure the property, and deal with problems. You have legal responsibilities, such as ensuring the safety of gas and electrical appliances and you should know your landlord and tenant law. You have to maintain the property, which may mean keeping it empty (so with no rent income) while the work is carried out.

You may regard this as too much hassle and decide to employ a managing agent. In that case, you will pay around 10-15% of the rental.

Choosing a Mortgage

The right choice of mortgage is important. You will find a range of lenders, who will typically lend 65-75% of value for up to 25 years; you will be allowed to borrow on several properties, up to an overall cash maximum. The lender may want a letting agent's confirmation about the likely rent income; he may charge arrangement fees and will require the house to be insured. You will have to cover your own legal and valuation fees.

Lenders to the buy-to-let market recognise that you may spend time without tenants – 'voids' in the jargon – and so may allow you to make 10 payments a year rather than 12 and even take a six month payment holiday.

The experts' principal health warning is to avoid a high mortgage. If you assume that the house remains unlet for three months of the year and you have to reduce the rent by 10%, it is possible to show that you would start to lose money on a mortgage of 75% or more.

Two Approaches

There are two different types of investor in the buy-to-let market. The first will own a number of properties, the choice being based on background in the residential property market. For this investor, capital values will be of less immediate importance than that the rental income should continue. His portfolio will grow through selling for a profit and re-investing. The second type of investor will own one or perhaps two buy-to-let properties in addition to his principal residence. If he has bought in the centre of London or another major city, he will probably be looking for medium and long-term capital growth, aiming primarily to cover his outgoings in the interim. For people in this position it can make good sense to break the rule about buying a property you would like to live in: you can later sell your home, where the gain will be tax-free as your principal residence, and move into the property which you bought as a buy-to-let.

Capital Gains Tax – and a Solution

When you come to sell your buy-to-let house or flat, you will very likely face a bill for capital gains tax, after taper relief and acquisition/disposal costs. On a house or flat, you will be charged capital gains tax at your marginal rate of up to 40% (for a high rate taxpayer) which taper relief will gradually reduce to 24%. If this is a cause for concern, as it is likely to be for longer-term investors, one option is to focus your buy-to-let decision on holiday cottages.

The government classifies furnished holiday lets as a business asset – as part of its aim to stimulate the tourist industry. On business assets, capital gains tax is charged at only 10% for a higher rate taxpayer once the property has been owned for just two years or more. There are some fairly restrictive rules for these lets: the property has to be in the UK and available for letting at least 140 days a year. It must be let for a minimum 70 days a year and not occupied by the same person for more than 31 days.

Further Tax Posers

Running your buy-to-let as a business asset could also help to cope with a number of minor tax restrictions which are making life more difficult for buy-to-let operators. For example, the private landlord will find that the management of rental properties is not regarded as a trade for tax purposes. This means that landlords who have no other sources of income cannot invest in personal pensions because their property rents are considered to be investment income: under current regulations contributions into a personal pension must come from earned income (the only exception being the stakeholder pension, where contributions are limited).

There is also a bias against landlords who manage their own properties as opposed to using letting agents. But if you manage the property yourself, you may have an argument with the Inland Revenue on whether repairs and maintenance are improvements: this is an uncertain area, with all the difference between costs which are tax-deductible and those which are not.

Property shows every sign of remaining a sound long-term investment, but it goes through booms and slumps and, above all, is relatively illiquid. This means that someone putting £100,000 in the buy-to-let market should ideally have two or three times that amount in cash and securities – unless the buy-to-let is being run wholly as an income operation. And you are placing a large amount in one specific asset in one specific place: that judgment takes on considerable importance.

There are other ways to invest in real estate, as opposed to actually buying it: you can buy property unit and investment trusts and you can invest in property bonds. (You can even place bets on future property values through specialist City firms – but this is perhaps a minority interest.)

Property Unit Trusts

Around the turn of the century, when equities were sliding, the typical property unit trust out-performed the market. Property unit trusts have direct exposure to property and to shares in property companies. They have an advantage over private investors in being able to access commercial property which tends (subject to location) to be less volatile than the residential market. Commercial property yields – looking at the mix of industrial, commercial and office real estate – tend to be higher than residential and to offer a margin over gilt-edged and bonds. Central and local government and major companies, such as the banks, represent low-risk tenants for property companies, while commercial property compared with residential appears less in the political limelight.

Some of the property unit trusts have grown large and there are also a number of property investment trusts. Successful gearing is especially important for a property investment trust, so you should look at the discount to asset values (up-dated so far as possible) and the record.

How to Invest in Higher House Prices

The outstanding performance of house prices over the years, as against equities and bank deposits, has led to the creation of property bonds. These are aimed at people who believe house prices will keep rising, who are prepared to lock up £5,000 or more for 3-5 years with the guarantee that their capital will be returned. The bonds are usually linked to the Halifax house price index, often with no upper limit. You can invest for 3-5 years and will be offered 100% or 120% (i.e. a higher rate of interest) of the rise in the price index. The index appears monthly, is based on all houses and is not seasonally adjusted.

One important point to check is whether the gain comes as income or capital; practice varies, with capital likely to be more attractive to investors. One advantage of these bonds is that you can invest through an ISA: you can transfer existing ISAs and PEPs and you can invest direct as well. Normally the final index level will be averaged over the closing twelve months.

The immediate appeal of these bonds is that your capital is safe: your initial capital is guaranteed. But you have to face tying up a significant amount of cash for several years. If house prices fall over the particular period, or just fail to rise, then you will have incurred an opportunity cost: over five years a competitive instant access account should have earned around 20%, with your capital also safe. Property bonds are meant to be held for the full duration of the term; you may be able to cash in early, but it is likely to cost.

Giving to Grandchildren

Those of us who are retired and have grandchildren like to give them presents. Why not give a financial present – which has the added merit of being tax-efficient?

When parents give money to their children, any interest above £100 a year is taxed as the parent's: from the standpoint of the Inland Revenue, what matters is not the name in which shares or a deposit are registered, but who donated the capital. Gifts made by grandparents, indeed by anybody else, are free from this restriction. Avoid confusion: if a gift is made by someone other than the parents, but the holding is registered in one or other of the parents' names, you should keep a record of the origin of the funds.

For children born after September 2002, there will be further scope through the government's new Child Trust Fund ('Baby Bond'). This will give every child a £250 endowment at birth (more for poorer families) and allow parents, relatives and friends to add up to a further £1,000 a year. The Fund will become the child's property at age 18, to use how he or she wishes. Full details should be available in late 2003, though no funds will transfer until 2005.

What Should You Give?

One obvious choice is an ISA, but this cannot be given to a child under 18 – or 16 for a cash mini-ISA. As a grandparent you can give cash to one of the parents to hold in an ISA – which is tax-efficient – but that will reduce the parent's ISA allowance.

Part of the total gift should probably be in cash, which can be placed for the grandchild in one of the higher-yielding ready access accounts. The important point here is that children each have their own personal allowance for income tax and capital gains tax.

Pensions v Shares

When stakeholder pensions were introduced, some interesting calculations were made of how much a fund would grow – thanks to help from the Chancellor – if you invested the maximum of £3,600 gross or £2,808 net for 18 years. (See the section on stakeholder pensions, page 114.) The theory was that the child could then take over the plan at age 18 and carry it on until, say, age 60. This plan would give the child a flying start towards its own pension portfolio, and compound growth over 18 years does produce some impressive statistics. But one has to believe that the child may have more pressing needs – to pay university costs, buy a first home – and the stakeholder pension cannot be cashed in until they reach age 50.

The alternative, given that one is looking at a time-scale of 18 years or more, has to be equity investment. A specific share poses problems – who knows what the corporate world will look like in a quarter of a century's time? – so the answer has to be a low-cost unit trust, such as a tracker fund with an accumulator facility; an investment trust is an alternative. This will avoid the need for the parents to cash a dividend twice a year and re-invest it – though they will, on behalf of the child, reclaim the tax deducted from the dividend payout.

How to Give

The short, and effective, answer is to give unit trusts using a bare trust (explained on page 159). This requires a minimum of organisation and you simply designate the investment for the child. The investment is then regarded as belonging to the child, which is clearly important in order to obtain the allowances, and the child can only gain access to the money on reaching adult-hood at age 18. You can postpone this date by other arrange-ments, say until the child reaches age 25.

One final thought: consider a fund which might interest your grandchild – an ethical fund, a technology fund or one for emerging markets.

Giving to Charity

Most of us want to give to charity, and this is recognised in the taxation rules. There are concessions to charitable gifts in both inheritance tax and capital gains tax (see those sections, pages 37 and 27) and especially in income tax.

The income tax concessions in particular point towards more effective ways of giving to charity – but also contain one or two pitfalls.

Making the Gift

For anyone who remains employed, the most effective way of giving is through the company's payroll. This may be run by your employer, or by an organisation such as the Charities Aid Foundation, which operates Give As You Earn. The money is deducted from your pay and passed direct to the charity, and the scheme is free from restrictions. For the rest of us who are retired and no longer have access to an employer's scheme, the most effective way of giving is through Gift Aid. We all hand over cash to flag collectors and others, but Gift Aid is so much more effective for everyone concerned.

How Gift Aid Works

Under Gift Aid, you get relief at your highest rate of tax on your donations to charity. Your gift is treated as payment from which basic rate tax has been deducted, and the charity can reclaim the basic rate tax back from the Inland Revenue. If you pay tax at the higher rate, then you get further relief to set against your income.

There are some points of procedure you should be aware of. These concessions apply to approved charities, so unless you are giving to a well-known charity, it might be sensible to ask for the charity registration number which it will have been given by the Charity Commissioners.

From your side – to enable the charity to reclaim the basic rate tax – you should send the charity a Gift Aid declaration. Keep a record of the declaration you send the charity so that you can reclaim tax relief.

Gift Aid Arithmetic

An example is the simplest way to show Gift Aid in action, but the charity needs to resolve one issue first – especially if your gift is paid under covenant. As we have said, if you give £100, that is treated as £100 net so the charity reclaims £28.20 which is 22% of the grossed up gift of £128.20.

But there is an obvious trap here for the charity: if standard rate of tax is reduced, its income will fall. It is equally true that its income will improve as standard rate is increased, but the trend – which most of us hope will continue – has been for the standard rate to fall. For this reason some charities have asked for gross amounts; in this case, if you agreed to pay £100 gross, then you would send the charity a cheque for £78. If standard rate were to be reduced to, say, 20%, then you would have to send a cheque for £80. In this way, the charity's income is maintained and you in effect bear the cost of the reduction in standard rate tax.

Gift Aid is extremely flexible, and there is now no minimum or maximum on the amount of donations which can qualify.

A Warning to Taxpayers

When you fill in a Gift Aid declaration, many charities will ask you to state that you pay sufficient tax to cover the relief you have deducted (if it is gross) or which the charity will reclaim from the Inland Revenue (if it is net). This is in fact for your own protection: the Inland Revenue will claim money from you if you don't pay enough tax to cover the payment to the charity. Suppose that you sent the charity a donation for £1,000; this is treated as net and the charity will claim £282 from the Inland Revenue. But if your tax bill for the year came to only £200, you would have to pay over the difference of £82.

There is a clear and important point here: where a couple make payments to charity, those payments should be made by the one who pays the higher rate of tax. And if one of you is losing some age allowance because your income is above the starting level, gifts to charity can be doubly helpful; Gift Aid donations are deducted from your income when it is assessed for age allowance.

Covenants

In earlier years, covenants were the principal way in which people gave money to charities: a covenant is a legal agreement to make a series of payments and they were written to last for four years or until some later event, such as ceasing to support the charity. A large part of the total given to charity is still made under deeds of covenant, which have now been simplified.

For one thing, tax relief now runs on and does not expire after the four years. Covenants started before April 2000 now come under the Gift Aid scheme. For covenants after April 2000, you have to supply a Gift Aid declaration in order to claim tax relief. For the charity, the covenant provides the important comfort of being able to rely on receiving income for a period of years.

If you are making substantial donations under covenant, you need to be aware if the charity is using funds for non-charitable purposes or sending them overseas without ensuring that the money will be used for charity. This may not be very likely, but if it does happen you may find that your own higher rate relief is restricted.

Gifs of Shares

Giving to charity by donating parcels of shares is covered in the section on capital gains tax (page 27), but the point is so important as to be worth briefly re-stating. Rather than donate out of income under Gift Aid, you could give the charity shares on which you are showing a large capital gain. If you do that, no capital gains tax is payable and the value of your donation is used to reduce your income for tax purposes (note that it offsets income, not other liabilities for capital gains tax).

If you hold a parcel of shares which is showing a loss, you should sell the shares for cash and so realise a loss for capital gains tax. You should then give the cash to the charity, and the amount will go to reduce your taxable income. If you simply give the shares to the charity you will miss the opportunity to establish a loss to set against your capital gains.

Don't Give Cash – Use Gift Aid

The conclusion has to be that you should use Gift Aid rather than handing over cash or using your credit card. It is not only better for you, it is much better for the charity. Two essential rules: you need to keep copies of your Gift Aid declarations and you need to be sure that you are paying sufficient tax to meet the claim the charity will make. If one of a couple is a higher-rate taxpayer, then he or she should take over the covenant payments. Charity giving is good; financially effective charity giving is even better.

Credit Cards

Most retired people have a credit card; many will have two or more. Credit cards have become immensely popular over the last 40 or so years, but one wonders: are they being used wisely? A large part, some £50 billion, of the massive consumer debt relates to credit cards, where the rates can easily be four times the Bank of England base rate or more. It does not make good sense to work out a financial strategy and then go in for high-rate fixed interest borrowings.

Managing Your Debt

Credit cards are an extremely convenient way to handle purchases: they defer the cost, by up to eight weeks, and they offer some useful collateral benefits (see below). Nor are they especially difficult to obtain. The alternative way to buy goods and services is to use cash, a cheque, or a debit card.

Accepting that credit card debt is costly, how do you manage it? One way is to make sure that all outstanding balances are paid off each month; this may sound like a counsel of perfection – but it would be more cost-effective to arrange a borrowing from your bank or a finance company and avoid getting into debt on your credit card.

Handling the Rules

You are now treating your credit card as a sort of spending programme. The first question to consider is fee; some credit and charge cards levy a fee but many do not. Given that cards are used to defer costs, you need to assess how long a period of interest-free credit (which is what it amounts to) will be available? As a corollary, you will need to consider the level of service provided; while generally good nowadays, service does vary and is hard to assess except by word of mouth – and by your own experience!

The same logic applies when you consider what rewards you can expect for using the card. Some issuers offer a useful benefit, for instance, of making no extra charge for overseas transactions – which many issuers levy from cardholders. There are a number of cards which offer benefits such as airmiles or points which can be redeemed at specified retailers, or to meet certain bills or to buy a car. Several credit cards offer a cash handback, generally once a year based on say 1% on all transactions (not cash withdrawals) or 0.5% on an initial amount rising to 1%.

What Sort of Card?

Before making a final decision, you need to be clear which type of card you want. 'Credit cards' is a term often used loosely, but there are good reasons for being precise and distinguishing a credit card from a charge card and a debit card. A credit card means what it says, i.e. that it gives you the facility to pay by instalments rather than settling the whole balance at the end of each month. A charge card does not offer this facility, so that there is no credit element. A debit card is simply a means of moving funds from your bank account, so again no credit element arises.

Your choice will depend on a number of factors. corporate cards tend to be charge cards which are paid off every month. Many people own a debit card because it is a no-cost way of getting cash from an automatic teller (ATM or 'hole in the wall') or because some suppliers charge an extra 3% or so if they are offered a credit card.

Case for Credit

There is a strong case, when making a large purchase, for using a credit card – the perhaps too little known Consumer Credit Act. So long as the price of the item you bought was more than £100, the credit card company as well as the retailer is liable for any breach of contract. This means that you can claim against the retailer and the credit card company for faulty goods or services. And the facility is particularly useful when your supplier goes bust. If you had paid money to the retailer, by way of a deposit, for example, you are unlikely to get it back nor will you get any compensation. But you have the fall-back of being able to go to the credit card company. The normal procedure, if a problem arises in this sort of case, is to write to both supplier and credit card provider.

One point to remember: it is not completely clear whether the Consumer Credit Act applies abroad, though that seems to have been the official intention and many credit card companies accept that.

Legal Issues

This is not intended to replace legal advice, much less suggest you become a DIY lawyer. But there are a number of legal issues involved in financial strategy, and it is important that you understand the basics.

Make a Will

Making a will is an important step, which a surprising number of people fail to take. When you make a will, your estate will go where you want, as opposed to following the rules of intestacy. If you are concerned to save inheritance tax, then it is essential to direct where your assets go. At present, the beneficiaries of your estate have two years in which to re-write your will under a deed of variation, which must carry the agreement of all those who lose out under the new arrangements. This could be useful for you as a beneficiary, but for many years past people have been expecting the government to end this facility – and one day they may do it.

When you make a will, you need to review it every three to five years. Your assets may change, as may the law and your own family situation. Choosing executors is something you should discuss with your family and probably a solicitor; your chosen executor may die or become incapacitated at the same time you do. So think of something like the partner in your firm of solicitors, and in his absence someone nominated by the senior partner of the firm, or their Trust Corporation. You can nominate, say, two competent members of the family – but nominating individuals, as opposed to a firm, carries a risk. People die, emigrate, fall ill – sometimes just at the time when they are most needed. Banks also offer executry services, but their charges are often on the high side.

Powers of Attorney

One of the sadder features of ageing is that people lose their faculties. Where people are mentally fit, but physically unable to collect their pension, they can nominate an agent to collect the money for them. (Under the new rules, this can be done on a regular basis but not on the odd occasion.) When the mental faculties suffer – maybe temporarily – an appointee can be named to make claims and receive benefits: often this is a relative who lives with or visits the person concerned.

The next stage is to arrange a power of attorney, which can be general, or specific or time-related. You may have given one to your solicitor when he bought or sold a property for you; if you go on a long holiday you may give a power of attorney to someone so that a takeover offer can be accepted for one of the companies in which you own shares, or that you don't miss the opportunity when a company makes a rights issue.

... And the Enduring Sort

Powers of attorney are simple and widely used – but they are valid only so long as the person is capable of giving instructions. If the person giving the power of attorney becomes mentally incapacitated, the power comes to an end.

This is the very time when a power of attorney is most needed, just when it cannot be given. As the years go by, you should think of giving an Enduring Power of Attorney, which means what it says – that the attorney will be able to take complete control of the person's affairs. This EPA has to be registered with the courts; this may happen straightaway, but must happen when the attorney believes the person is starting to lose mental skills.

Many people go through life without giving an EPA – maybe it has never been suggested, maybe it looks too intimidating. But the longer you live, think about it: you may lose your mental skills because of a sudden accident or illness. Without a proper power of attorney, your friends and relatives will be just about able to cope – but it will take time, a number of people's energy and it will cost. In the ordinary way you should appoint two of your children to be the attorneys, as there are problems if a sole attorney dies.

Using Trusts

Trusts have two principal purposes – to assist in tax planning, especially inheritance tax, and to restrict people to whom you want to give money from getting their hands on it straightaway, as for example, if they are too young.

Trusts are very much an area for the specialist and if you want to explore the possibilities you should contact an accountant or a solicitor. But as with powers of attorney, you will find it helpful to know the possibilities, at least in outline – if only so that you can better understand the sort of advice you are being given.

In inheritance tax planning, the essential point is this: by placing a financial asset, such as an insurance policy, in trust, you put it outside your estate for inheritance tax. And putting assets into trust is not at all a complicated business: often the insurance company or other financial organisation involved will enable you to do so with minimum fuss and cost.

Some Types of Trust

Types of trust which you may encounter and find useful are:

BARE TRUSTS

These are often offered by unit trust groups for instance when you, as grandparent, are setting up investments for children. The units belong to your grandchildren but they do not take control until they reach 18, the age of maturity. This is the traditional way of giving funds to children where they can't get access to the money immediately. A gift to a grandchild is a potentially exempt transfer, so that you have to live for seven years to escape IHT – and if you are giving shares or units rather than cash, work out the capital gains first.

WILL TRUSTS

Trusts can also be set up using your will. A discretionary will trust is often created when the husband accepts advice to leave the nil band to the children – so saving the amount of inheritance tax which will ultimately be paid – but is concerned that his widow may then be short of assets and income. The useful feature of such a trust is that the surviving spouse can be included as a beneficiary along with the children, their spouses and grandchildren; the widow retains access, via the trustees, to the funds which are transferred to the trust. There is a saving of IHT, while the survivor can still benefit from the late spouse's assets.

DISCRETIONARY TRUSTS

These are the most flexible type of trust, where the trustees have complete discretion over the allotment of the income or capital. You can provide for your surviving spouse and for grandchildren who do not yet exist. But these trusts are the prime case where inheritance tax has to be paid before death: if gifts to discretionary trusts exceed the nil rate band (take care if you are making other lifetime gifts) then you have to pay at half the normal IHT rate, i.e. 20%.

ENDOWMENT TRUSTS

These are one of the simplest ways to reduce the impact of IHT. You set up a series of single premium endowments with staggered maturity dates and the whole investment is placed in trust. As the policies mature they go back to the donor, but all policies which have not matured by the date of death will fall outside your estate for IHT purposes. But – this represents a potentially exempt transfer, so that you have to live for seven years for the plan to become fully effective.

Chapter 6:
Solving Problems

Beating the Market

Schemes that will beat the market – or break the bank – are as old as markets themselves. But assume that you looked for a scheme that would give you above-average performance – rather than trying to outdo the market at all times. We expect above-average performance from professional fund managers – i.e. we expect their funds to do better than the relevant stock market index – and some succeed over a period of years. If this is your objective, consistently to do better than the average, then perhaps there are strategies that will help.

Here are two strategies as candidates. Both of them require input from the investor, in the sense that you will have to accumulate information all of which is public but not all of which is readily available from the press or the internet. In the investment world, as in others, quality input tends to generate corresponding output. All of these strategies involve equities only.

High-yield Portfolio

Buying high-yield shares has a long record of out-performing the basic stock market averages by a useful margin. Just why this works is not wholly clear – it may be that a high yield works as a defence if the share price comes under pressure; it could be that a company moves from high yield to low yield – i.e. its capital value improves – when its good qualities are recognised. But whatever the reason, over the last 10-15 years a high-yield portfolio has outperformed the stock market average.

You have first to decide your benchmark for what represents a high yield from an ordinary share. You could take the prevailing

Bank of England base rate, or twice the average yield offered by shares in the market index.

CHOOSING THE SHARES

At first sight, this looks easy. As you glance down a list of shares in the newspaper or a stockbroker's analysis, there are a number which meet that test. But some of these shares will be in small companies, where volatility is high. So your first test is to restrict your choice to larger companies, say the top 250 or 350 in the market.

Next, you should look at the company's record. You should be able to see a progressive dividend record, of dividend increases over the last three to five years. You want to avoid a company with a static dividend record, where the shares have declined to give an above-average yield which does little more than reflect the market's continuing disappointment.

CHECKING THE PROSPECTS

You need to access market analysts' forecasts for the current year – these are available in the press, on the internet or from brokers who specialise in following the particular share. You should see from forecasts that the dividend is likely to be increased, which is important for two reasons. First, it indicates that profits are moving upwards; secondly, it suggests that the company's financial position is sound, so that it will not have to keep its dividend down in order to save cash.

By checking the market view of prospects, you will also avoid a classic share price trap: a company's share price falls because the stock market believes that trading and/or cash has deteriorated, so that the dividend may have to be cut. If that happens, the yield on the shares will appear high because the published yield calculation is based on the previous year's total dividend.

DIVIDEND PROTECTION

Finally, you need to examine how safe is the dividend. The basic test is how many times the dividend is covered by the available after-tax profits – put another way, what proportion of earnings is being paid out to shareholders? You should look for cover of at least 1.5-2 times, so that an upper limit of two-thirds of profits are going to shareholders. You need to spend some time examining dividend cover: in some sectors dividend cover is traditionally low, such as banks and retailing, whereas in manufacturing and pharmaceuticals cover is normally higher.

The main reason for these different cover levels is the expected rate of capital expenditure, so you should look at the accounts to check that the company's capital spending is within the amount of its depreciation and cash flow.

THE HIGH-YIELD SELECTION

You should now have a list of half a dozen or so high-yield ordinary shares. You have gone through the financial tests; all that remains is your personal assessment of the particular companies and their prospects.

Once you have completed that assessment you have your high-yield equity portfolio. On the historical data, from now on you should out-perform the stock market average.

Risk Analysis

A second strategy to beat the market average is to assess the risks of certain shares, or even groups of shares. This is very much an American technique, which will appeal to the more skilled investor. The objective in analysing risk is so that you can strike a balance between risk and reward; improving this balance should also improve the overall performance of your portfolio.

BETA FACTOR

Beta factor is a term you will see widely applied in stockbrokers' research to specific shares or even to fund managers' portfolios. A share's beta factor is based on historical evidence – how much of the changes in the share price result from changes in the overall level of the stock market.

The beta factor is expressed as a number: a beta factor of 1 means that the share is expected to move in line with the market. A beta factor of 2 means that the share is expected to be twice as volatile as the market overall.

ALPHA FACTOR

Alpha risk measures that part of total return which is relevant to the company, i.e. which does not depend on the market as a whole. Alpha measures the risk which attaches to the particular equity.

Alpha and beta may sound academic, but they are widely followed by professional fund managers in the US and the UK. They bring immediate practical applications: suppose that you hold shares with high beta factors – then if you want to move more closely in line with the market as a whole, you should choose other shares with a low beta, probably not more than 1. Suppose that your portfolio throws up high alpha factors – in other words, you can expect volatility from your shares quite apart from market movements. In that case, you are entitled to expect larger rewards from your more volatile portfolio, under the familiar trade-off between risk and reward. If your shares are not performing above average, then you are running risks without corresponding reward. In other words, you can reduce your risk exposure – by buying shares with lower alphas.

HISTORY – THE GUIDE

Many people who use the beta-alpha analysis find that it helps to improve portfolio performance. The assumption behind this risk analysis is that the beta and alpha ratings do not change rapidly, so that one can safely rely on recent historical data.

On that assumption the jury, as they say, is out. Anyone holding telecom shares during the first six months of 2000 will have witnessed dramatic changes in companies' risk factors. The dot.com boom and bust may be an extreme case, but this analysis would be much more difficult if risk factors were to change over the short term.

HOW MUCH VOLATILITY?

When looking at your overall portfolio, you need to reach a decision on how much volatility you can accept. For someone age 60, the suggestion is that you have a fixed interest-equity split of 60-40. That may look sensible, and you may accept the long-term case for equities as opposed to cash and fixed interest.

This may all be true, but we know that equities are by far the most volatile investment: equities may out-perform all other investments over a five and ten year time-frame but in the intervening years shares can rise or fall easily by 15% or 20% a year. If you have successive obligations to fulfil, or simply a spending pattern that needs to be financed from investments, the only solution is to enlarge the fixed interest element beyond the 60-40 spread.

There is a clear cost: if you enlarge the fixed interest element, your portfolio is likely to under-perform the 60-40 split over five or ten years. The experts would draw a distinction here between risk and volatility. Risk, in its basic sense, means that you may lose all or part of your investment. Volatility implies that you have a sound investment, whose value fluctuates because of outside causes. If you need to realise your investments, and cannot just shrug off a downturn, your volatile investment has become risky – you may even be facing a loss.

The moral: set out your liabilities over your retirement and if necessary change your assets accordingly.

Endowments Which Don't Pay Enough

There are more than 10 million endowment policies in the UK; more than half of these may well fail to meet their objective – to pay off the holder's mortgage. Perhaps six million people are facing a shortfall on the debt which relates to their home.

For the many people in this situation, there is one golden rule: take action and take it quickly. Waiting will not help – and it is your own home which is involved.

Falling Rates

The first step is to understand why this has happened. The story will be all too familiar to investors who have held shares, zero preferences and with-profit bonds. The falling stock markets of the late 1990s, with lower inflation and lower interest rates, have led to a massive decline from the heady days of the late 1980s.

Because the decline takes place year-on-year the severity of the impact may be less obvious. But if you compare, for example, average payout values for a ten-year endowment over the period 1991-2002, you will see a drop in returns of 30%; average yields have halved from 14% down to 7%.

Equities v Gilts

These falls have not been uniform. Insurance companies which originally invested in equities have tended to do better than those which preferred gilts and fixed interest over recent years. One of the further complications for policyholders has been that different companies have performed very differently.

For a 25-year policy, which would be usual for house purchase, the highest maturity value was about double that of the worst. In a number of cases, a holder with two policies would have one which was on target with the other warning of a shortfall – bringing the understandable reaction: if insurance company A can do it, why can't company B?

Three Letters

Knowing how the problem arose is useful, but the pressing issue is what should you do? The starting-point is the 'reprojection' letter which your insurance company sends to you indicating whether your investment is on track to repay the mortgage.

These letters are colour-coded: a green letter means that your policy is on track to repay the mortgage, though the policy must grow by 6% a year – the level of stock market growth which the Financial Services Authority tells policyholders they should now expect – if a shortfall is to be avoided.

If you receive an amber letter, then you are being told that there is a significant risk your policy is not on track to repay the mortgage. If the letter is red, the message is that there is a high risk of your being unable to repay your mortgage when the endowment policy matures. In a typical case, 4 out of 10 letters are green, 3 amber and 3 red. But one suspects that the proportion of amber and red letters may even be increasing. All of these traffic-light coloured letters will state facts and should include a helpline number.

Action

The universal advice is that, even if you receive a red letter, you should not panic but you should take early action. If this is new to you, the Financial Services Authority itself offers an advice booklet. The heart of the problem lies in the third or so of endowments which have to grow by 8% a year, which looks a demanding target – some major insurers have promised to pay the full expected return provided that markets grow by at least 6% a year. Policies with 10 years or more to run offer holders a chance of making up lost ground; policies which mature within five years are likely to need remedial action.

Four Choices

INCREASE THE PREMIUMS

Assume that you have received a red letter and that you have formed a rough idea of the likely shortfall. The first thing you can do is to increase the premiums on your policy. This is a simple and relatively inexpensive course, assuming that the policy still has a number of years to run. You should not have to pay further fees, and at the very least this will buy you some time: if conditions were to continue to deteriorate for another several years – possible, but perhaps less likely – you may have to think again. If conditions improve, then you can expect some surplus. But even if you are convinced that things will get better, it makes sense to cover the shortfall: you are dealing with your own home, and you could be wrong.

TAKE OUT A NEW POLICY

The second course, as an alternative to higher premiums, is to take out a new policy, perhaps of a different term from your original policy. That may be more costly than paying higher premiums – because of the expenses loading during the early years – but a new policy can give you more flexibility.

INVESTMENTS A POSSIBLE ANSWER?

Not many people, it has to be said, advocate higher premiums or a new policy on quite understandable grounds. An endowment policy got you into this difficulty, so why add to it? The third course is to set aside an investment portfolio to meet the shortfall. You will look for a low-risk portfolio with reasonable growth prospects – two ideas are better-quality zero preference shares or a corporate bond ISA with the income ploughed back into the fund. If you are looking out five years or more, the compounding effect of the corporate bond ISA will be useful.

You may go to the other extreme and decide that endowment policies are no longer for you. The objection is that you may be cashing in at a low point, maybe even the bottom, of the market. But if that is your decision, you should sell your policy, where you can expect to get around 30% more than if you simply surrendered it back to the insurance company; you will need to pay off or re-finance the loan.

OR A NEW MORTGAGE?

The advice most often given to someone facing a shortfall is to re-mortgage: that should have the useful benefit of cutting your effective rate of interest. If you sell the policy, you can re-mortgage on a repayment mortgage where you pay off both interest and debt each month. (This compares with an interest-only mortgage, where you just pay the interest each month.) If you decide to keep the policy, you should take out a repayment mortgage which will cover the shortfall at the end of the policy period.

Under this route you are formally recognising the shortfall but you need to be aware that your outgoings will be increased. The repayment mortgage will impact on your cash flow: you may want to consider extending the term.

Are You a Victim of Mis-selling?

Several insurance companies have been fined for mis-selling endowment policies, and some consumer groups believe that perhaps half of endowments have been mis-sold. But first things first: deal with your shortfall.

Many thousands of people have claimed that they were mis-sold endowments, and just under half of these have won their case and received compensation. But you must remember that disappointing performance is not the same as mis-selling. To make a case for mis-selling you will have to show:

❖   The policy was unsuitable at the time it was sold.
❖   You were not made to understand the nature of the product you were buying, or the nature of the risks involved, at

the time you bought your policy.

❖ The transaction was inappropriate given your personal and financial circumstances at the time.

Next Steps

If you feel that you were a victim, then your first step is to write to the company or to the organisation which sold you the policy. If you ask for compensation and this is denied, or if you are unhappy with the way your complaint is treated, then you can go to the Financial Ombudsman Service. But before you do that, you should have received a final response to your complaint – or silence for more than two months.

And it goes without saying that if you embark on this course you must keep a copy of all letters, together with notes of telephone conversations and you should use recorded delivery.

Solve the Shortfall

But even if you were a victim of mis-selling (if you win, the compensation will be the difference between the performance of your endowment policy over the period and a repayment mortgage) you should not delay in dealing with the shortfall. This shortfall represents a potential debt on your home, and once you are put on notice that there is, or there may be, a problem then you should deal with it. Never forget: a debt on your home can put your home at risk.

Getting Financial Advice

You can get financial advice in many ways. You can buy books like this; you can carefully read the weekend issues of the serious newspapers, together with the personal finance sections of the serious Sundays. You should read them at least once a week, to keep up with your share or unit trust prices and to be alert to changes in the finance or tax regime.

You can also talk to friends, but having a friend as an adviser has its problems. You will be resentful when his advice goes wrong; he will be resentful that he was not given the full picture and that you took his advice perhaps only to a partial extent and some time in arrears.

Going to Professionals

There are, it is said, about 30,000 different financial products available. You may well feel, therefore, that you need to call upon some professional resources. Insurance companies are an obvious starting-point, but you will find that most of their representatives are tied to the company which employs them. Still, you may get some idea of what products are available – though the terms may differ among different companies.

Banks are a natural source of advice, and many of them advertise tax services and general financial advice. (You must appreciate, at this stage, that you are moving into the area of paying for your advice.) Your bank may well be prepared to help a substantial or long-standing customer but they will probably charge you for tax and related services.

Solicitors and Accountants

Solicitors are a natural source of advice, though their input is likely to be legal rather than financial. You will go to a solicitor to make your will – which you and your spouse should do – and to advise in the setting up of trusts. A solicitor should be able to help in the broad area of inheritance tax, though he will probably stop short of advising on particular financial products.

Many retired people will already employ an accountant. If you are self-employed, paying higher-rate tax or if your affairs are at all complex, you should probably go to an accountant. He can advise you, from his experience of many other clients, on what is likely to work and his audit of your affairs will be important in dealings with the Inland Revenue.

Both solicitors and accountants will charge fees, possibly into four figure amounts if your affairs are at all demanding. If you don't already employ solicitors or accountants, your former employer may be able to help; if you are self-employed, you have to ask around. Remember that professional firms have their specialities – solicitors who are good at conveyancing may not be so good at setting up trusts. And a good deal will depend on whether you are trying to solve a particular problem or whether you are looking for an overview of your financial affairs – in itself not a bad idea when you have just retired.

Financial Advisers

There are thousands of financial advisers up and down the country. They are governed by the law and regulated by the Financial Services Authority. You can find them in your yellow pages, or through their trade association while some advertise in the press.

Many investors will have dealt with execution-only advisers, who are formally not advisers at all. What they offer is low commissions, either in the form of cashback or extra units if you are buying a unit trust. You have to choose the product to buy or sell, and you may even be asked to confirm that you have not received any advice.

Changing Structure

The way advisers operate is in process of being changed. Under the old set-up, advisers were either tied or independent. Tied advisers offered advice only on the products of one company or group of companies. Their charges were usually low and they had a useful role, when you were already invested with a particular bank or insurance company, in being able to guide you to a more cost-effective product. The role of the independent adviser was to offer "suitable advice". People tended to choose them by function – say if you needed pensions advice – or by location: it makes sense to employ an adviser who is accessible to you and the trade association can supply names of advisers near where you live or where you specify.

"De-polarisation"

Many people regarded the division between tied and independent advisers as rigid and unhelpful. Hence the jargon term "de-polarisation" or ending this divide. The new plan, as put forward by Sandler in mid-2002, is to have just one class of IFAs (Independent Financial Advisers) who would charge fees, not commission – some people believed that advisers had been tempted to put forward those financial products which paid them high commission. (Having urged de-polarisation, the authorities and the FSA seem to have back-tracked: some commissions will be permitted, if the investor agrees.)

Alongside the IFAs would be financial product distributors, who would operate as salesmen for financial products: for example, they would be able to sell stakeholder products to the public, where no advice was offered and no mis-selling allegations could arise.

Meeting the Adviser

You have chosen your adviser and agreed to meet for an informal talk which will not carry any commitment on either side. The association's literature says rather disarmingly "There's no reason why you have to really like your adviser . . ." but you have to respect his judgment and to establish a good working relationship: it is probably best to have some regard for your adviser.

Before you meet the adviser for the first time, you need to verify some basic facts. You need to know how long he has been in business. You need to know what qualifications he has: the basic qualification is the Financial Planning Certificate.

Your First Talk

You are happy with the data you have received and you want to go ahead. You go to your first meeting.

The adviser will charge you a fee (maybe subject to VAT, which makes a difference) on which you need to agree. An industry guideline is up to £200 an hour, with the rates tending to be higher in London and the south-east. Fees should always be specified and agreed before any work is done.

Your adviser will be receiving income on financial products which you buy and where commissions will arise. These amounts can be substantial, so you need to establish in advance what rebates are possible and how they will be accounted for.

The theory is that, as you pay fees for your advice, the adviser will be able to choose freely between products which offer him high or low commission.

How it Works

Your next need is to explore how the relationship will work in practice; here the advisers' trade body offers some good ideas for questions. You should ask whether the firm specialises, or which are its stronger areas. You should find out whether you will always deal with the person you are talking to – if there are other advisers involved, you need to meet them. And you have to know what happens if your named adviser is away when you have a pressing investment question.

Some women prefer to have access to a female financial adviser, and your initial guidance from the trade body will make clear if this is possible.

Telling All

From an adviser's point of view, the most difficult situation is to be asked to advise when he only knows part of the story. To get the best out of an adviser, you need to give him a full account of your financial position together with your plans and ambitions for the future and your financial thinking in the context of the family – your plans for your children and grandchildren.

What you tell the adviser will be written down and you may be asked to verify that the information is correct. Before you contact an adviser, you need to prepare all the information he will need. The more complete the information, the better his advice should be. You may decide to ask for advice only on specific aspects of your finances; that makes sense, but you need to work out before the meeting exactly what you want him to advise on.

Finally, do go to the meeting with your spouse, or partner or main beneficiary.

Choosing a Broker

Time was when someone retired, who wanted to trade in shares, he would go to a small firm in the City. In the late 1980s the High Street banks moved in – but now they are being massively under-cut in price by execution-only brokers, who hold clients' shares electronically and who operate over the telephone, and most cheaply of all over the internet.

Execution-only

These new types of brokers do not offer investment advice; they simply buy and sell what you tell them. Some of them will provide, or arrange to provide, an advisory service but this will be separate and will be charged on a different basis. Advisory brokers tend to start at 1.9% on small sales, execution-only brokers are around 1% while the new internet brokers will offer a fixed amount per transaction which will probably be less than 1%.

Paperless Shares

One feature of the new brokers is that they hold your shares electronically; there are no share certificates. This enables them to speed up the process, especially as regards settlement and so reduce the costs. Dividends can be paid straight into your account. You may also have noticed that many unit trusts act in a similar way – send you a contract note while telling you that your units or shares will not be certificated.

   One immediate point to watch is whether the broker charges you for holding shares electronically on your behalf; the practice varies, and it is not difficult now to find a broker who will hold your paperless shares without cost. You also need to check whether he will charge you if you decided one day to move your portfolio to another broker.

   Some people do not feel happy with paperless shares – though it is now becoming more expensive to hold and deal in paper certificates. There are specific issues: you need to make sure that your paperless shares entitle you to receive accounts, vote and qualify for the shareholder benefits which some companies provide.

Trading New Style

The new brokers operate in a similar way to their traditional predecessors, while they may offer you a wider choice of action. You can buy or sell 'at best', when you leave the broker to get the best terms for the deal you have decided to carry out. You can trade with a limit, when you set the price below which you will not sell and above which you will not buy. You can deal 'at quote' when the broker gives you a price and you have a very short time in which to decide whether or not to accept.

The other costs of a transaction will be the usual ones – stamp duty of 0.5% on purchases and a £1 fee to the City of London Takeover Panel if you make a trade which is valued at more than £10,000.

Savings – The Attraction

The attraction of the new-style brokers is clear: you will make big savings on your share trades. Compared with the offshoots of the High Street banks, you could save around £100 even when making only five or six trades a year. If you trade once a week, the savings could be more than £500. Finding one of these brokers is not difficult: some advertise, and you can find details in the weekend financial press and investment magazines.

You may not have access to the internet; many of the new brokers also offer a telephone service, at a modest premium to their on-line facility. You may have a problem, as has been indicated, over shareholder benefits (see page 134); in that case, it may make sense to keep those particular shares – which in any case you will be planning to retain rather than sell – in certificate form outside the electronic nominee account.

Perhaps the more fundamental problem is that these brokers are execution-only; you will not receive any advice. But in any case you will either be taking your own decisions or following an independent financial adviser.

The ending of paper certificates represents a big change on previous practice, but many other organisations are following this route. For the majority of people, the substantial cost savings will be simply too great to ignore.

Changing Your ISA/PEP

People who own PEPs and ISAs hardly ever change them; once they have bought their ISAs, investors seem to put them away. Out there – maybe even among readers of this book – there are many people with seriously under-performing investments.

The figures are staggering: the amount invested in PEPs is between £40 and £50 billion, say £1,000 for every adult in the country. Yet a recent survey by the Unit and Investment Trust

Association showed that in one recent year less than 5% was switched.

Why Change?

The first reason to change your investment is that it is not performing. (Some people may be under the illusion that if you change your PEP or ISA investment, then you lose your tax-free status: this is not true.) No sensible investor would assess under-performance over a short period; the literature suggests that you should think of an investment over five years, and this probably makes sense.

But there may be considerable under-performance, which is why people should change their PEPs and ISAs – and change has now been made relatively simple. To assess under-performance, consider an analysis carried out by a leading firm of financial advisers. This looked over a five year period at the performance of funds by sector, taking the best fund, the average sector performance and the worst.

In UK Equity Income, the best growth was 120%, the average of 17 funds was 42% and six funds – some with well-known fund management groups – came out below 20%. In UK All Companies the best was 114%, the average of 47 funds was 34% and no less than 18 funds could not manage even 20%. And this 18 included funds managed by well-known banks, stockbrokers and insurance companies.

Things Can Go Wrong

One's first reaction is to wonder how things can go so drastically wrong. It may be a change of manager, an error in strategy (which evidence suggests, matters more than stock selection) or the fund grew so fast that it became difficult to manage. But the reasons, interesting though they are, matter less than the result: there are many under-performing funds, and some of them are managed by the best-known names in the industry.

That represents the first reason why you should think of changing your PEP or ISA. In addition, your own needs will change over the years; you may well want to move from an All Companies fund to Equity Income or Corporate Bonds. Another good reason for thinking of change is that the rules of

PEP investment, in particular, have been greatly widened. Initially, investors were largely restricted to the UK or European stock market but this is no longer the case, so that now the US is a possible outlet, along with Japan and South East Asia.

From a practical standpoint, you may want to consolidate and thereby simplify your holdings. Previously, if you held six PEPs with different managers you would receive 12 valuations during the year, probably at varying dates which made it difficult to keep a perspective of how your investments were performing. You could simplify the position by investing with just two or three managers, but that involves extra risk. Now, changing your investments has been made much easier.

How to Change

It is fair to say change has been made easier, but it would be too optimistic to say that it has been made easy. There are some official-based rules:

❖ You may not transfer current tax year maxi ISAs to mini ISAs and vice versa.
❖ You may not transfer between components of an ISA.
❖ If you have invested in a maxi ISA in the current tax year then your investment must be transferred in full.

The great change has been brought about by the rise of the on-line supermarkets. These operate in a similar way to discount brokers, and rebate some or all of the commission they receive from groups for selling their products. The difference from discount brokers is that the brokers offer only an execution-only service: you, the investor, have to know what security you want to buy. The fund supermarket equally does not offer advice but it does provide a great deal of data so that investors can choose, and some supermarkets offer packages of funds which are aimed at specific types of investor. Some supermarkets deal direct with the public, though others will deal only through intermediaries.

Observation – and Slow Consolidation

The first moral is to watch the performance of your PEPs and ISAs. It is sensible not to act for a five-year period, but the evidence suggests that there are many portfolios aged well over five years which are lagging behind the indices.

Whether or not you decide to stay with your existing investments, it makes sense to consolidate: you will be saved a good deal of paperwork and, above all, you will be able to form a clear overall view of your investments' performance. Unless you have some pressing requirement to move, you will probably find it more practical to consolidate gradually. You could time this change to coincide with a move to a new fund manager.

How to Borrow

Not very long ago a banker stated that 'no-one over the age of 60 needs to borrow money'. His remark provoked a swift and contrary reaction. His customers and potential customers pointed out that the over-60s have a wide range of borrowing requirements, such as a second home, that long-awaited holiday or unplanned expenditure. Few people should be surprised that the over-60s are no exception in a nation of borrowers: right across the country the average debt per adult is around £25,000 of which about two-thirds will represent a mortgage. (Total consumer debt is now over £800bn and has been growing fast.) The over-60s have some advantages: their mortgages will be partly, if not wholly, paid off, they will have established (one hopes) good borrowing records and their income, largely pensions, is secure and readily forecastable. But they suffer from some disadvantages: many finance markets are geared to younger employees or the self-employed.

Mortgages Still the Cheapest

Expected borrowings are the easiest to deal with and mortgage rates remain among the lowest of borrowing rates. Most of the over-60s who still have mortgages will have paid off a part, so that one easy way to borrow is to enlarge and/or extend the mortgage. (Incidentally, anyone who still has a mortgage should look at re-mortgaging, perhaps employing a mortgage broker; the savings can be considerable.) To take out a new mortgage may not be easy for the over-60s, though a bank loan can be structured with a mortgage as security. The government is looking at long-term fixed rate mortgages, which have so far lacked consumer appeal.

Personal Loans

For people who are not suited to a mortgage, and are deterred by the rates charged on credit cards, the most likely option is a personal loan. These loans are offered by most banks and can be geared – though not necessarily – to a significant purchase such as a car or a major piece of household equipment. Personal loans are short- rather than medium- or long-term, with three years probably the most common period; anyone wishing to extend can take out a further loan either with his original lender or another. Personal loans are often not secured.

Interest rates on personal loans tend to be somewhat higher than on mortgages, but rates are not the whole story. Some lenders charge fees while others insist on payment protection in case of illness. If you are looking round the market for a personal loan, you need to look at the comparative monthly repayment figures rather than rely on a simple interest rate assessment.

Overdrafts

These are the traditional forms of bank lending, which in theory were short-term and self-liquidating. If you were self-employed before retirement, you may well have set up a business overdraft facility – but you may not find that easy to duplicate in the post-retirement world; the banks would probably point you in the direction of a personal loan. But an overdraft is highly flexible and remains worth exploring, particularly if you have a need for funds over the next year or so which will fluctuate from month to month and whose amount at any one time cannot be forecast with accuracy. Rates tend to be close to those for personal loans.

Two points are worth remembering at this stage. Security could be useful in obtaining a personal loan or an overdraft, both in improving your chances of success and getting a lower rate. The security needs to be reasonably generous (at least from the bank's standpoint) and publicly identifiable: a typical case would be the security of a share portfolio worth 150% of the personal loan or the maximum overdraft. If your shares are jointly owned, your spouse will have to consent and some types may not be capable of being used as security. The second, simple but too often forgotten, point, is that you may take a five-year borrowing but if repayments start immediately, the effective life of the loan will be that much shorter; in planning your repayment timetable, this can make a big difference.

Specialist Lenders

A number of companies operate, especially through press and television advertising, which offer to cut down your various outgoings into one simple monthly payment. This is normally done by the company paying off your debts, probably credit cards, and taking a charge on your house. They will charge for this, though the interest rate will probably be lower than you were paying before. The catch is that the new borrowing will be secured on your house: if you get into difficulties on this borrowing, as you did on your previous debt, then you risk losing your home.

In many cases, it would make more sense for you to take out a three-year personal loan, pay off all the other debts, and use the breathing-space to work through a plan of debt reduction.

Count the Cost

Borrowing, except perhaps for house mortgages, is not necessarily cheap and cannot be set against tax, unless you are self-employed and borrowing for business purposes. You need to pay attention both to the monthly cash outgoing and to the interest rate you are being charged: many people are not sensitive to interest rates and in particular to compound interest. Remember this: if you borrow at 7%, then the amount you owe will roughly double every 10 years; if you borrow at 10%, then your debt will nearly double every seven years. Borrowers need a book of compound interest tables, or at least a calculator.

Two Important Don'ts

There are two extremely important don'ts in borrowing. Don't go over your agreed overdraft limit or your credit card ceiling, and don't be late, even by a day, in making agreed repayments –

assuming that they are not organised by direct debits from your bank, which they probably will be.

There are three principal reasons why you should stick rigorously to the borrowing agreement. First, you will be charged horrendous rates of interest for the excess and possibly a fee on top. Second, if you fail to adhere to the letter of the agreement, you may even find that the lender can walk away from the agreement as well as charge you a penalty. Third, if you don't keep to the terms of your agreement, you may start to acquire an adverse credit record and that is something you do not want.

... And Some Remedies

If you do get into difficulties over your repayment schedule, contact the lender beforehand. Start over the telephone, and make a note of the conversation; write to the lender the same day confirming what had been agreed over the telephone. If despite all this you encounter problems, or the lender tries to charge penalties in spite of the agreement, you may have to pay under protest (this depends on the wording of your agreement). You can then write to his compliance officer and if that fails (or he does not reply after eight weeks) then you can go to the ombudsman. Never forget that borrowers, too, have rights.

A Rainy Day

You always have to allow for the unexpected: in financial terms, this means keeping some of your assets liquid – which means available at short notice without capital loss. That points to a bank account, either instant access or at seven days' notice, or to a money market or roll-up fund: these can normally be cashed after a few business days' notice. The problem with being liquid is that the returns tend to be low – you have to pay for accessibility – and over the years your assets will suffer from inflation.

There is no conventional wisdom as to how much you should keep liquid. If you are aged 60, you will probably have 60% of your investments in fixed interest form. Maybe one quarter or one third of this, 15-20% of your investments, could be liquid: this is very much a matter of personal taste and judgment. What you should do is look around carefully (using the press and the internet) before you place your money; your benchmark should be an after-tax return which keeps up with inflation.

... Which May Turn Stormy

To many people, it is just plain common sense to keep some assets readily available. What concerns many pensioners is the prospect of a major adverse shift in the external economy – perhaps even back to the difficult days of the late 1970s and early 1980s. Future problems probably won't replicate the past, but the difficult question is: how do you deal with a rise in inflation, when a large part of your assets are in vulnerable fixed interest securities?

The test would come once inflation started to rise above the government's specified level of 2.5%. There are two things you could do. One is to become a borrower – assuming that you are able to obtain reasonable rates. In times of inflation, it is almost always better to be a borrower than a lender – as the real value of your debt is reduced by rising prices. For pensioners, this would point to borrowing on mortgage or one of the equity release schemes.

Look Abroad

The second way to defend your assets against inflation is to hold a part of them in non-sterling investments. Bank deposits and roll-up funds can easily be switched into dollars or euros and there is little difficulty in buying US or continental government bonds. The theory here is that inflation in the UK would weaken sterling against other currencies – in principle, by the amount of the excess inflation.

Rainy days apart, there is a basic investment case for having some international spread of your investments – the UK represents a small part of the world economy, though you should never lose sight of the basic fact that you, and your obligations, are located in this country.

Index-linking

Index-linked assets are an obvious candidate for a rainy day portfolio, and you can buy either index-linked gilt-edged, or index-linked savings certificates which have a two- or five-year life. Any retired man or woman who is concerned about possible future inflation should invest in one or other of these: the gilt-edged offer low real yields and there is a relatively small amount in issue, and hence are probably best left to the professionals. Index-linked certificates are easy to buy and you can hold up to £10,000 in each of the two issues. These certificates offer a small yield over inflation, which is paid on maturity.

Pension Problem

If a high rate of inflation were to return – which, at the time of writing, looks very unlikely – most people would suffer, except those who had index-linked pensions. (Even they would suffer to some extent, because of the time-lag taken to adjust the pension – which, one assumes, would also affect the State pension.) Company pension plans would often cover the first 5% of inflation, but not necessarily beyond that. A sharp divide would emerge, between former private sector employees and pensioners who had worked for the State sector and so enjoy index-linked pensions.

If high-level inflation were to return, it would be essential to act quickly. A return to the 1970s-80s would not take place overnight. If you believed inflation would return, you should take action.

Useful Addresses

Association of British Insurers
51 Gresham Street
London EC2V 7HQ
Tel: 020 7600 3333
www.abi.org.uk

Age Concern England
Astral House
1268 London Road
London SW16 4ER
Tel: 020 8765 7200

Age Concern Cymru (Wales)
4th Floor
1 Cathedral Road
Cardiff CF11 9SD
Tel: 029 2037 1566

Age Concern Scotland
113 Rose Street
Edinburgh EH2 3DT
Tel: 0131 220 3345

Age Concern Northern Ireland
3 Lower Crescent
Belfast BT7 1NR
Tel: 028 9024 5729

Association of Investment Trust Companies
Durrant House
8-13 Chiswell Street
London EC1Y 4YY
Tel: 0800 085 8520
www.aitc.co.uk

Banking Ombudsman: contact Financial Ombudsman Service
(see below)

Building Societies Association
3 Savile Row
London W1S 3PB
Tel: 020 7437 0655
www.bsa.org.uk

National Savings and Investments
Blackpool FY3 9YP
Tel: 0845 964 5000
www.nsandi.com

Office of the Ombudsman for Estate Agents
Beckett House
4 Bridge Street
Salisbury SP1 2LX
Tel: 01722 333306
www.oea.co.uk

Financial Ombudsman Service
South Quay Plaza
183 Marsh Wall
London E14 9SR
Tel: 0845 080 1800
www.financial-ombudsman.org.uk

Financial Services Authority
25 The North Colonnade
Canary Wharf
London E14 5HS
Tel: 0845 606 1234
www.fsa.gov.uk

Help the Aged (England)
207-221 Pentonville Road
London N1 9UZ
Tel: 0808 800 6565
www.helptheaged.org.uk

Help the Aged (Wales)
Room 123
CSV House
Williams Way
Cardiff CF10 5DY

Help the Aged (Scotland)
11 Granton Square
Edinburgh EH5 1HX

Help the Aged (Northern Ireland)
Ascot House
24-30 Shaftesbury Square
Belfast BT2 7DB

Inland Revenue: refer to own tax office or local directory

Insurance Ombudsman: contact Financial Ombudsman Service
(see above)

Investment Management Association
65 Kingsway
London WC2B 6TD
Tel: 020 8207 1361
www.investmentfunds.org.uk

Law Society
113 Chancery Lane
London WC2A 1PL
Tel: 020 7242 1222
www.lawsociety.org.uk

Law Society of Scotland
26 Drumsheugh Gardens
Edinburgh EH3 7YR
Tel: 0131 226 7411
www.lawscot.org.uk

Law Society of Northern Ireland
Law Society House
98 Victoria Street
Belfast BT1 3JZ
Tel: 028 9023 1614
www.lawsoc-ni.org

Pensions Advisory Service
11 Belgrave Road
London SW1V 1RB
Tel: 0845 601 2923
www.opas.org.uk

The Pensions Ombudsman is at the same address.
Tel: 020 7834 9144
www.pensions-ombudsman.org.uk

Index